THE KNOWN STRATEGY FOR STUDENTS

ARE YOU DEVELOPING STUDENTS OR YOUR STUDENT MINISTRY?

JEFF PRATT &
SCOTT STEVENS

LifeWay Press®
Nashville, Tennessee

ISBN: 978-1-4158-6891-1
Item 005271294

Dewey Decimal classification Number: 259.24
Subject Heading: STUDENTS \ CHURCH WORK WITH STUDENTS

Printed in the United States of America

Student Ministry Publishing
LifeWay Church Resources
One LifeWay Plaza
Nashville, Tennessee 37234-0174

We believe that the Bible has God for its author; salvation for its end; and truth, without any mixture of error, for its matter and that all Scripture is totally true and trustworthy.
The 2000 statement of *The Baptist Faith and Message* is our doctrinal guideline.

CONTENTS

JEFF PRATT is the Director of LifeWay Student Ministry Training and Events. Through the years he has served on church staffs as pastor, church planter, and student minister. Jeff currently serves as the student minister at First Baptist Church Nashville.

Jeff became a Christian while in college at Carson Newman in Jefferson City, Tennessee. While there he wrestled, earned All-American honors and represented the United States in 1985 in Greece, Paris, and Yugoslavia.

Jeff and his wife Julie have one young adult and two teen-aged children—Cole, Madison, and Alec.

SCOTT STEVENS, Ph.D., is the Director of LifeWay Students and leads the team responsible for LifeWay's ministry offerings for teenagers, their families, and their leaders—including resources, camps, events, and training. He has over 25 years of student ministry experience and has served as a volunteer leader, a part-time and full-time student minister, and as a student ministry professor.

Scott is married to Debbie, and has two children—Tanner, age 16 and Annie, age 12. Their family attends Forest Hills Baptist Church in Nashville where he volunteers in the middle school ministry.

INTRODUCTION

THEN & NOW

NO MATTER WHAT you call them—teens, teenagers, youth, students, young people, or adolescents—ministry to people between the ages of 12 and 20 has evolved over the past 200 years. After more than two centuries of church and parachurch ministry focused on this segment of the population, what is the primary focus of today's ministry efforts toward teenagers? Is the focus on matters essential to their spiritual development, or have distractions crept in as ministry to teens has become increasingly specialized over time? Before exploring answers to these questions, let's take a look back to see how significant developments from the past have contributed to the current state of student ministry in the United States.

The Past: Creation of an Adolescent Subculture

The Industrial Revolution.—The greatest single contributor to the creation of a youth subculture in the United States (and in other countries) was the Industrial Revolution of the early 19th century. As families moved off their farms to work in the factories of growing cities, children were no longer needed as essential components of the labor force. In fact, as work in the factories became more dangerous, Congress enacted child labor laws that prohibited the employment of children.

So, what do you do with all these formerly-employed young people? You educate them. Another significant contributor to the dawn of the youth subculture was mandates from both state and federal governments requiring compulsory education for those between the ages of 6 and 18. The first public high school in the United States opened in 1875. As school participation increased, the local school became the primary crucible for the mental, emotional, and social development of young people.

The motives for removing children from dangerous work environments and inserting them into educational settings were certainly noble and resulted in improved opportunities for young people. However, one of the unintended consequences was that these decisions began to systematically separate young people from their parents and much of the adult world. These subtle steps began to radically change the expectations placed on young people. No longer would they rapidly move from puberty into adult responsibilities, but rather there would be an increased time of transition between childhood and adulthood. In 1904 G. Stanley Hall was the first to describe this transition period as "adolescence."

Puberty.—Speaking of puberty, there have been some significant changes in this life-altering, hormone-driven, body-changing phenomenon over the last 100 years as well.

For one, it is occurring earlier and earlier for boys and girls. During the mid-1800s the average age of puberty for girls was between 15.6 and 16.5 years of age. Today that age is 12.5 years, with some girls beginning puberty at even younger ages.[1]

Guys are also experiencing puberty at younger ages. In 1900 the average age of puberty for guys was 14-16. By the late 1900s it was 12-14.[2] This "secular trend" has been attributed to increased body weight (especially fat levels) in children, hormones in beef and milk, increased chemicals in food, and even sexualized messages targeted to teens through the media. Teenage guys are taller, heavier, stronger and faster than they've ever been.

Coupled with the earlier onset of puberty is the fact that young people are waiting longer to get married. The average age of first marriage has moved from the late teens and early twenties back in the 1800s, to age 27.1 for men and age 25.3 for women today.[3] It should also be noted that in the 1800s, marrying soon after puberty was influenced by a shorter life expectancy. Thanks to medical advancements, life expectancy increased and infant mortality rates decreased. Because there was no longer the pressure to marry young and immediately start a family, people began to delay getting married.

When these factors are combined, no wonder there is increasing sexual pressure on teens. Their early-maturing bodies are equipped and primed for sexual activity at younger and younger ages while the "approved" time (at least for Christians) to engage in sexual activity (marriage) continues to be delayed. Our sex-saturated society only adds to the challenge.

Juvenile Justice.—The creation of the juvenile justice system in the late 1800s also helped to create boundaries around the adolescent experience. Authorities began to believe juveniles should not be held to the same standard as adults in regards to criminal activity. Early reformers instituted separate legal proceedings for young people that continue to develop to this day.

Economics.—The economic realities of adolescent consumerism are staggering. In 2006, they spent over $179 billion in the United States—guaranteeing continued celebration of this group by marketers and the companies they represent.[4] As some have stated, teens have become "professional consumers" and parents have become "professional providers."

Delayed Adulthood.—When the darker side of adolescence is examined—crime, violence, teen suicide, teen pregnancy and sexually transmitted diseases, drugs, anger, and so on—one observer points to the creation of adolescence as a major negative force: "For the first time in human history, we have artificially extended childhood well past puberty. Simply stated, we are not letting our young people grow up."[5]

Formation of youth ministry organizations.—So, over the years, how has society chosen to impact the lives of young people as they navigate this extended path between childhood and adulthood? Statutes and institutions were created to protect them, but what opportunities were provided to help them develop into adults who could contribute to society? More specifically, as the adolescent years became a distinct period of life transition, what efforts were begun that focused on the spiritual development of young people?

Combining a love for God and a love for young people, many adults took proactive steps to provide ministry, education, and care for teens:

- The founding of Sunday School by Robert Raikes in Glouchester, England, in 1780.
- The creation of the YMCA and the YWCA in the 1840s and 1850s.
- The development of church auxiliary groups and societies for young people.
- The rise of parachurch groups such as Young Life, Youth for Christ, Student Venture, and the Fellowship of Christian Athletes in the 20th century.

These organizations and churches proved that young people were a viable ministry target and that attention to their spiritual growth was important. These ministries called young people to a deeper walk with Christ and helped to produce many of the key Christian leaders of the 20th century. (For more information on the development of youth ministry organizations see *When God Shows Up: A History of Protestant Youth Ministry in America* by Mark H. Senter III, [Baker Academic, 2010].)

We've taken a look at how our current adolescent subculture was formed and at some of the significant issues that teens wrestle with during these years. We've also glanced at a brief history of ministry initiatives focused on them over the past 200 years. Next we'll examine the current state of student ministry.

The Present: Great Opportunities and Significant Challenges

GREAT OPPORTUNITIES

There is no doubt that today's teen culture and the continued focus on students by Christian groups is providing unprecedented opportunities for significant ministry. Consider the following factors.

Growth of student ministry positions, compensation, tools, and training.—Student ministry has experienced tremendous growth over the past 30 years. There are more full-time student ministers, more churches with designated leaders for student ministry, and more colleges and seminaries offering student ministry training than ever before. The compensation and tenure of student ministers have increased. In addition, more organizations than ever are offering camps, curriculum, and other events and resources. According to findings by LifeWay Market Research & Intelligence, student ministry in the American evangelical market is a $730 million per year business.

A growing student population.—According to Magazine Publishers of America, from 1990 to 2000, the teenage population (ages 12-19) rose from 27.5 million to 32 million. It is expected to reach 33.5 million this year (2010). What an opportunity for ministry!

A diverse generation.—Thirty-three percent of teens belong to a minority racial or ethnic group. The Hispanic teen population continues to explode (4.6 million) and is expected to be 62 percent larger by 2020.[6] How diverse is the population of your student ministry or your church? Teenagers today are more likely to have a friend of a different race or ethnicity than ever before. Our student ministries and churches should reflect the same openness.

A growing pool of youth leaders.—More and more people are working with students in a lead role. According to the 2003 Southern Baptist Annual Church Profile, there were 22,561 people working specifically with students in a leadership capacity. These ministers were: volunteer, bi-vocational, interim, part-time, and full-time leaders. By 2008 that number had grown to 23,426. In roughly 45,000 Southern Baptist churches, at least half of them reported having a designated leader responsible for their church's ministry efforts to students.

These factors reflect a growing emphasis on ministry to students. We have moved past the era where youth leaders were seen merely as "directors of wildlife" or crowd-control agents. Families and churches have experienced the value that authentic ministry can bring to their students. So, how are we doing with these increased opportunities? Are we moving forward in ministry effectiveness?

SIGNIFICANT CHALLENGES

Advances in many areas of student work have also been met with significant challenges when it comes to their cumulative ministry impact. Time, effort, and money are being spent, but it seems that the overall results have been mixed. Here is part of what is being discovered related to ministry effectiveness.

Mythbusting Research.—As student ministry has matured and become more specialized, there have been a growing number of research studies about its effectiveness.

One prominent study is the National Study of Youth and Religion (NSYR). (See *www.youthandreligion.org/research.*) The Southern Baptist data from this study was distilled into *Transforming Student Ministry: Research Calling for Change* (LifeWay Press, 2005). The following are some of the key findings and conventional wisdom "myths" that were busted by the study:

☐ *Conventional Wisdom:* Teenagers typically rebel against their parents and other adults in their lives and thus reject the faith of those adults.
▶ *NSYR:* The lives and faith of most teenagers closely reflect the lives, faith, culture, and institutional settings of the adult world they inhabit.

☐ *Conventional Wisdom:* Teenagers raised in Christian homes and the church have a pretty fair understanding of their religious beliefs.
▶ *NSYR:* The vast majority of teenagers are incredibly inarticulate about faith and practices and their meaning or place in their lives. They find it almost impossible to put basic beliefs into words.

☐ *Conventional Wisdom:* Church teenagers understand that God is intimately involved in every facet of their daily lives.
▶ *NSYR:* Teenagers are "functional deists." They believe God exists, created the world, and set life in motion—but the only time He becomes involved with them in a personal way is to make their lives happier or to solve some problem.

☐ *Conventional Wisdom:* Church teenagers have resisted the influence of those who want them to be politically correct and "tolerant" in all their religious conversations.
▶ *NSYR:* Teenagers are incredibly well-trained in using "correct" language so they will not offend anyone in public. Away from church they cannot bring themselves to say that Jesus is the *only* way to God.

☐ *Conventional Wisdom:* Evangelical teenagers have a fairly good understanding of grace or the basics of salvation.
▶ *NSYR:* There is strong evidence that many evangelical teenagers do not understand grace or the basics of salvation.

☐ *Conventional Wisdom:* Teenagers in the church are no different than teenagers out in the community.
▶ *NSYR:* Despite its weaknesses and lack of influence, religious practice does indeed make a clear significant difference across all standard measurable outcomes in adolescents' lives.

These research findings began to raise warning flags for many who value and participate in student ministry. Could these facts be pointing to the need to re-evaluate our ministry paradigms? What else can we learn about our current effectiveness?

Decline in Student Baptisms.—The last year Southern Baptists baptized 100,000 teens was 1980. The 1992 Southern Baptist Annual Church Profile reported that churches baptized 92,032 students. In 2008, the number dropped to 75,215 student baptisms. Over a 16-year period, annual student baptisms dropped by 16,817! That number concerns us. It has to concern you too.

Church Dropouts.—According to the Church Dropout Study conducted by LifeWay Research (*www.lifewayresearch.com*) in 2007, 70 percent of young adults ages 23-30 stopped attending church regularly for at least a year between ages 18 and 22. That means 7 out of every 10 seniors who graduate from our youth groups also "graduate" from the church! The remaining 30 percent of adults ages 23-30 remained in church during those years, although with varying levels of frequency.

A summary of the current state.—The preceding information describes a variety of factors and results that are contributing to the current state of student ministry—some good and some bad. Let's summarize:

On the positive side:

- ☐ There are growing numbers of students in our country with increasing ethnic diversity.
- ☐ There are large numbers of churches that are ministering specifically to students.
- ☐ There are increasing numbers of leaders, resources, events, and training available for student ministry.

On the negative side:

- ☐ Spiritual depth and maturity among students is lacking.
- ☐ Student baptisms are not keeping pace with the population growth.
- ☐ Large numbers of students are "graduating" from church when they graduate from high school.

So what's our next step? How do we move forward to improve spiritual outcomes in the lives of our students?

The Future: A Focus on Student Spiritual Development

It seems that we've gotten pretty good at developing student ministries. The assumption over the past 35-40 years has been that if we develop quality student ministries, we will, in turn, develop great students. But it's obvious there's a problem. Our current methods are not working.

THE KEY QUESTION

Over the years an adolescent subculture has developed and student ministry has grown. Students face significant life issues and ministry programs, events, and resources abound, but spiritual results seem to be lacking. We cannot continue to do student ministry the same way and expect different results. This leads to the key question:

As student ministry continues to mature, are we developing students or our student ministries?

In other words, has student ministry become increasingly sophisticated at the expense of the spiritual transformation of students? How can this be remedied? Does the Bible offer any principles that can help us focus on the spiritual development of students? How can we maximize the spiritual impact of our efforts in ministry with students, their families, and our churches and communities?

The purpose of this book is to answer those questions. In the pages that follow we'll look at biblical foundations, strategy, and practical processes that can help you concentrate on student spiritual development. Thanks for taking the time to stretch your thinking about ministry with students. We have great love, respect, and admiration for people like you who love God and love teenagers. We are inviting you to join a movement of student ministry leaders:

- who have a passion to see students come to Christ and follow Him in baptism.
- who are willing to make needed sacrifices in their ministry approach for the sake of seeing students grow spiritually.
- who are committed to helping students stay plugged into the church for a lifetime.

Our prayer is that this book will encourage you in the ministry to which you have been called.

[1]Allen Jackson and Dwayne Ulmer, *Introducing the 21st Century Teenager* (Nashville: LifeWay Press, 2001), 27.

[2]Ibid.

[3]2005 U.S. Census.

[4]"What's New with Teens: TRU 2007 Key Findings," Teenage Research Unlimited (*www.tru-insight.com).*

[5]Robert Epstein, *The Case Against Adolescence: Rediscovering the Adult in Every Teen* (Sanger, CA: Quill Driver Books, 2007), 5.

[6]"Hispanic/Latino Market Profile," Magazine Publishers of America (*www.magazine.org/marketprofiles*), 11.

CHAPTER 1

A BIBLICAL FOUNDATION FOR STUDENT MINISTRY

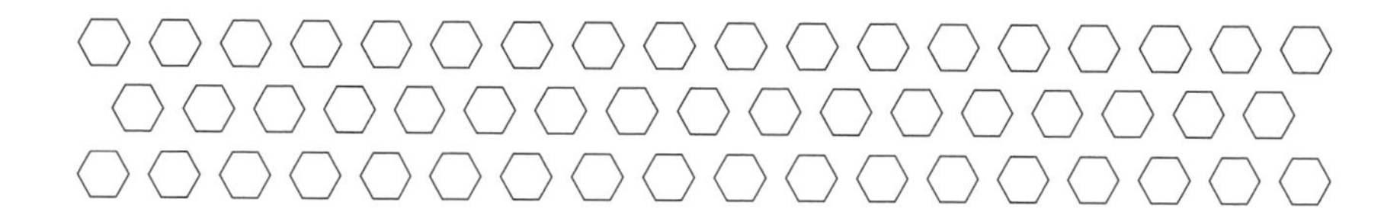

WOULDN'T IT BE NICE if the Bible provided a clear, delineated plan for ministry with teenagers? Such a plan would satisfy those who want a step-by-step guide to follow that would produce predictable results in the lives of the students we care so much about. As far as we can gather from our reading of the Scripture, no such plan exists.

Some have suggested, however, that Jesus was actually the first youth minister. Think about it: Jesus had 12 guys in His youth group (now recognized as the optimum size for a Bible study class). They often struggled to understand what they were being taught. (One guy was always blurting out answers, and one turned out to be a delinquent traitor!) Does this resonate with your experience? In fact, some believe that Peter, James, and John comprised the first youth council and that the experience on the Mount of Transfiguration actually occurred during the first youth council retreat.

Though it might be fun to consider other analogies between Jesus' disciples and members of your youth group, and though there is not a student ministry blueprint in the Bible, God's Word does offer us some foundational truths on which to build an effective ministry with teenagers. Let's take a look at some of these.

The Great Confession

When Jesus came to the region of Caesarea Phillipi, He asked His disciples, "Who do people say that the Son of Man is?"

And they said, "Some say John the Baptist; others Elijah; still others, Jeremiah or one of the prophets." "But you," He asked them, "who do you say that I am?" Simon Peter answered, "You are the Messiah, the Son of the living God!"

–Matthew 16:13-16

The central question for the world is, Who is Jesus? Peter answered the question correctly. He identified Jesus as the promised Messiah and God's own Son. And take note of the punctuation at the end of his statement: an exclamation point! Peter was convinced of the truth that God had revealed to him and did not shy away from making a declarative statement about Jesus' identity.

The Christian life begins with a Great Confession, and the very bedrock of an effective student ministry is found in creating opportunities for teenagers to understand who Jesus is. They must be exposed to all of His glory—past, present, and future—and given opportunities to confess His true identity for themselves. This can be challenging for student ministry leaders for a couple of reasons.

First, many students see Jesus primarily as a friend who exists to help them when life gets difficult—a buddy they can always count on. This has been referred to as the "Jesus in my pocket" view: I have Jesus in my pocket, and I can pull Him out whenever I'm going through a rough time and He will "be there" for me; otherwise He can ride along while I live my life. Christian Smith, through his research in the National Study of Youth & Religion, described teenagers as "functional deists." Smith states that teens believe God set the world in motion, but the only time He becomes personally involved with them is to solve a problem or make their lives happier. This view of our Lord falls woefully short of comprehending the majesty and authority of Jesus.

Second, students are quite adept at affirming a wide diversity of religious views simultaneously. The concept of tolerance seems to have morphed over the years. In the past, tolerance meant that people could hold opposing views on a particular subject and that they had the right to hold on to their divergent views. What has changed is that, while it's still accepted for individuals to hold to differing viewpoints, they must also affirm the opposing viewpoint as equally valid. The penalty for not doing so is to be labeled "intolerant" or even worse—"judgmental."

One of the last things teens want to be accused of is being judgmental, and one of the best ways to suffer this fate would be to make a declarative statement about the identity of Jesus to their peers. For some, the name *Jesus* remains one of the most offensive words in the world. Equally insulting would be to point to the Scriptural affirmation that there is only one way to God and that the path must go through Jesus. For many teens, especially away from the friendly confines of the church, it is almost impossible for them to say that Jesus is the *only* way to God.

During Jesus' earthly ministry there were many questions about His identity. He was performing miracles, challenging preconceived religious ideals, and speaking with an uncommon authority. In the midst of much confusion, God revealed to Peter the true identity of His Son, and Peter responded with a faithful confession of this revelation. Students need that same opportunity today.

The Christian life begins with a Great Confession.

The Great Commandment

And one of them, an expert in the law, asked a question to test Him: Teacher, which commandment in the law is the greatest?" He said to him, "Love the Lord your God with all your heart, with all your soul, and with all your mind. This is the greatest and most important commandment. The second is like it: Love your neighbor as yourself. All the Law and the Prophets depend on these two commandments."

–Matthew 22:35-40

In His reply to a question from a religious expert, Jesus wrapped up all of the teachings of the Mosaic Law (Genesis through Deuteronomy) and all of the writings of the prophets into three primary relationships:

- We must love God with all of our hearts and all that we are.
- We must love ourselves as we grow to understand who we are in Christ.
- We must love our neighbors as we live out our faith in God.

Interestingly enough, each of these relationships depends on the other two—they are inseparably linked. Each relationship is foundational to the spiritual development of teenagers and must be a fundamental emphasis in a biblically-sound student ministry.

Jesus' words reveal the primacy of loving God with every fiber of our being. In His answer to the lawyer, He quoted a portion of the Shema (Deut. 6:4-9), a passage that any Jewish person would have been taught from childhood. It seems that Jesus is saying we must focus both our affection and attention on God. Is that a struggle for you or the teens you know? It certainly is for us.

It boils down to a matter of priority. We all tend to focus on the things that are the top priorities in our lives. If there is some place we want to go, something we want to buy, or something we want to do; most of the time we will make the sacrifices necessary to achieve our priorities. We see it in the lives of students who invest tremendous amounts of time and energy to achieve academic and sports excellence or to conquer the latest video game (which is now played online with peers from across the street and around the world).

Jesus is saying that our top priorities should be to love God and love people. I (Scott) wonder how many examples our students have seen of people who love God with all they have and all they are? My fear is that most of them have seen hurried and worried adults who, more often than not, simply give God a nod while moving on to the next item on their agenda. Teens need real-life examples of complete devotion to Christ.

I also wonder how often teens see examples of people who love others as themselves. In research on youth ministers I conducted a few years ago, I discovered that while the group overall scored high in terms of their relationship with God, they scored lower than expected on their relationships with others. I'm convinced that a major contributor to being able to love others, for both adults and teens, is a proper understanding of our identity.

Identity formation is one of the key tasks in adolescent development. Students need to come to a confident understanding of who they are and why they are in the world. This best happens when they understand who they are in Christ. Teens need to know they were created for a purpose and have been given gifts, skills, and abilities to accomplish their life purpose. One of the great challenges of youth ministry and parenting is helping teens identify these gifts and then giving them opportunities to use them.

When teens have a confidence about their identity in Christ, they have an added resource to battle the powerful messages from the media and others that seek to speak to them about their identity. Did you know that most of the advertisements directed toward teens are for health and beauty items? With all of the focus on outward appearance, students desperately need attention on the inner qualities of character development.

The last part of the Great Commandment speaks of loving our neighbors. In today's world our "neighbor" could be next door, across our state, or around the world. Teens need encouragement and opportunities to live out their faith by loving their neighbors. We have seen that this is a generation that is willing to invest their lives in something they believe is worthwhile. Let's direct this natural energy and enthusiasm toward accomplishing the instruction of Jesus to love God and love others—the intersection of right belief and right action.

The Great Commission

Then Jesus came near them and said, "All authority has been given to Me in heaven and on earth. Go, therefore, and make disciples of all nations, baptizing them in the name of the Father and of the Son and of the Holy Spirit, teaching them to observe everything I have commanded you. And remember, I am with you always, to the end of the age."

–Matthew 28:18-20

When I (Scott) think about the concept of being commissioned, my mind conjures up images of men and women entering military service. There is a tremendous task ahead of them that will be dangerous and will offer both risk and reward. In a very real sense, they are about to enter a life and death battle that may require the ultimate sacrifice. As Jesus was about to return to heaven, He also gave His followers their marching orders in what has come to be known as the Great Commission.

He began by stating that He holds all authority in heaven and on earth. Shouldn't this fact increase our confidence to engage the task He is about to give to the church? Oftentimes I think we forget upon whose authority and whose strength we are attempting to accomplish the call of God in our lives. Let's rest in the fact that Jesus is in control.

Next He told us to go and make disciples (or literally, as we are going, make disciples). Wouldn't it be great if we could just "make" disciples? I am thinking of a supplement we could put in our water bottles or maybe some secret ingredients we could mix together, microwave, and then poof: instant disciple! Maybe this is why He tells us that making disciples will happen as we move through our lives—that it will take time to make a disciple.

Jesus continued His instruction by speaking of baptism and teaching. We commonly refer to these as the church functions of evangelism and discipleship. As we consider these biblical foundations for student ministry, we can never forget this foundational truth: Every teenager needs to know Jesus Christ. They need to know Him personally as their Savior and Lord, and they need to know and practice His Word.

So how are we doing? Well, how can I put this delicately?… We have much room for improvement. In the United States there are now over 30 million teenagers. Though the population rate continues to grow, the rate of students being baptized and/or participating in church continues to fall. The last year that 100,000 teens were baptized in Southern Baptist churches was 1980—over 30 years ago! And baptism numbers have continued to drop since that time.

Jesus also instructed us to make disciples of all nations. While there is growing ethnic diversity in the U.S. teen population, churches are not necessarily reflecting this trend. Progress has certainly been made in some areas, but much work remains. It seems like we are comfortable traveling to foreign countries or visiting distant cities and ministering to a variety of people, but bringing that experience home to our own church and community can be a different matter.

You'll notice that Jesus doesn't separate the functions of evangelism and discipleship. They are opposite sides of the same coin and a biblically-grounded youth ministry will include both. It can be tempting for those in leadership to overemphasize the area they are more comfortable with, but a balanced approach and emphasis is needed. Effective evangelism should lead to discipleship and vice versa.

Jesus concluded the Great Commission with an encouraging word for His followers: "I am with you always." If you are struggling today with feelings of frustration or defeat in your ministry with students and their families, remember that Jesus is with you. He has called you, equipped you, and placed you in a leadership position "for such a time as this." The unique constellation of your gifts and abilities and the needs of the students you are seeking to reach are a part of His plan. Enter the battle with His confidence.

Jesus' Development

And Jesus increased in wisdom and stature, and in favor with God and with people.

–Luke 2:52

The Bible doesn't give us a lot of detailed information about Jesus as He grew up, but it does provide some interesting facts. Here's a quiz for you. What is the first recorded word of Jesus in the Bible? It is the word *why*. That's right, as a 12-year-old, speaking to His parents, in church, the first recorded word of Jesus in the Bible is *why*. Of course this was after His parents had been searching for Him for a few days following the Passover Festival in Jerusalem. You've got to love the description of their response to the replies given by their 12-year-old son, "But they did not understand what He said to them." Ha!

This should provide comfort for all parents who have ever struggled to understand the behavior of their children—especially 12-year-olds, and especially in church! But all humor aside, this verse does provide us some clues about what was going on during this period of Jesus' life. In fact, it is the only glimpse we have of the life of Christ between the age of 12 and when He began His public ministry some 18 years later.

The verse describes a process of development that occurred in Jesus' life over time. The Greek word used in

Luke 2:52 for "increased" is the word *prokopto*. It means *to drive forward, to advance,* or *to grow in time*. From the time He was 12, we know that Jesus was moving forward or advancing in His development. Jesus was 100 percent God and He was 100 percent man. As a man He developed physically, mentally, emotionally, socially, and spiritually. He experienced all the joys and challenges of the human condition. Let's take a look at these areas of development.

The first area He developed in was "wisdom and stature." The word "wisdom" in the Greek language is the word *sophia,* which means *the knowledge of how to regulate one's relationship with God, being prudent with others,* and *knowing how to regulate circumstances*. It also carries the idea of *spiritual insight into the true nature of things*. An important aspect of Jesus' development was His growth in understanding how to regulate His relationship with the Father and how that shaped His interaction with the world.

An example of Jesus' growing wisdom is found in Luke 2:46-47. These verses describe a scene in which Jesus was sitting in the Temple complex with the teachers listening, asking questions, and astounding them with His answers. The teen years continue to be an amazing time of mental maturation. Students move from concrete to abstract thinking, and the questions they ask can get a lot more complex! (Can I get an amen?!)

When it comes to growth in stature, have you ever wondered if Jesus had questions about His changing body as He grew from a boy into a man? What sort of conversations did His parents or teachers have with Him about these changes? Physical development is one of the most profound changes to occur during the adolescent years, and for some students these changes can be a little scary. Teenagers need honest information about what is going on with their bodies and the assurance that what they are experiencing is a normal part of growing up.

Emotional development was also a part of Jesus' experience. While we do not have information on this from His early years, there are many examples of Him expressing His emotions in the Scripture. Can you think of times in which Jesus revealed His anger, compassion, empathy, sarcasm, and sense of humor? The key here is that He never committed a sin in the expression of His emotions. One of the great tests of student ministry is both encouraging and modeling a healthy expression of our emotions.

A second area that Jesus developed in was "favor with God." The key to understanding this aspect of growth is to understand the usage of the word "favor." The Greek word for favor is the word *charis*. The word *charis* is the word *grace* in the English language, and it connotes *divine influence on the heart that is reflected in life*. The meaning refers to a favor done without expectation of return, the undeserved loving-kindness of God to men. Jesus did not grow in favor with God by earning His love but did grow in His understanding of what it meant that the Father had bestowed such an incredible gift on Him. It is a gift that is based singularly on God's heart as the giver and not on any effort or merit of the receiver.

If His later life is any indication, Jesus spent regular time with the Scriptures and with His Father in prayer as He grew up. Those are still the foundational disciplines that students need today. Every ounce of encouragement we can give teens is needed so they can recognize their need of the Savior. Once they have come to Christ, the focus of our student ministry efforts should be to help them forge an indispensable relationship with Jesus that will guide the rest of their lives.

A third area in which Jesus grew was in "favor with people." As He developed in His understanding of what it meant to be the recipient of His Father's great love, Jesus grew in learning how to become a grace giver to His fellow man. He essentially became what the Father had modeled for Him. This helps us see that development doesn't occur in a vacuum, but in the context of relationships with others. It is also a reminder of the inextricable link between our relationship with God and our relationships with others. One affects the other.

One of the more interesting elements of adolescent development to observe is in the area of social relationships. We wish we had a little more information on how Jesus related with His peers at the age of 12. We do have evidence that He related well to adults—both the teachers at the Temple and with His parents. Scripture indicates that Jesus was an obedient son. But how did He do with His friends, brothers and sisters, and so on? Being able to relate well with others remains a key element of the developmental process.

Luke 2:52 is a good reminder to us that teenagers are in a process of development. Each area of development is intertwined with the others and all of this is working simultaneously. Another truth worth remembering is that these students are in the process of becoming all that God has created them to be. They are not finished products, but incredibly valuable individuals. What a privilege to partner in their journey.

The Sermon on the Mount

What is the Scriptural content students need to grasp as a part of their spiritual development process? Well, it's the whole Bible! But is there a single passage or section that captures the core of biblical teaching, a section of Scripture that encapsulates key areas for spiritual development?

Our search landed on the Sermon on the Mount (Matt. 5–7) for the following reasons:

- It was the first recorded sermon of Jesus—an important message for all His followers.
- It interpreted much of the Old Testament teachings in light of Jesus' coming.
- It focuses on the motivation behind our behavior.
- From beginning to end, it covers a wide variety of life issues.
- It provides a framework for effective kingdom living.

A topical breakdown of the Sermon on the Mount provides a handy outline for focusing our thoughts on key areas of spiritual development for students.

Sermon on the Mount Topical Breakdown

▶ *Character:* Matthew 5:1-12 (The Beatitudes)

The Beatitudes provide images of character traits that should be descriptive of kingdom citizens. Humility, purity of life and purpose, power under control, and a deep longing for personal righteousness and corporate justice are just a few of these traits.

▶ *Influence:* Matthew 5:13-20 (salt and light)

Jesus instructed His followers to make an impact in the world. He told them to act as a preservative (salt) in helping to combat the decay of the world, while also reminding them that their good deeds are a reflection of their Father that will be noticed by men.

▶ *Relationships:* Matthew 5:21-48 (heart condition, love your enemies, and so forth)

Jesus zeroed in on our hearts as the source of the trouble in our relationships with others. In contrast to accepted practice, He told us to love our enemies and to extend ourselves in serving others.

▶ *Disciplines:* Matthew 6:1-24 (giving, praying, fasting, true treasure)

Spiritual disciplines, including the proper motive and practice thereof, are the focus of this section. Investment in items of eternal value is also stressed.

▶ *Lordship:* Matthew 6:25-34 (God's sovereignty; seek first the kingdom of God)

Jesus explained God's ultimate control of the circumstances of life as well as an admonition to spend more time focused on Him than on our daily worries.

▶ *Discernment:* Matthew 7:1-27 (the narrow gate, false prophets, the wise builder)

As Jesus brought the sermon to a close, He focused on making wise choices. He summed up the passage by illustrating the possible outcomes related to how His listeners choose to apply what He has taught.

The Role of Parents

"Listen, Israel: The Lord our God, the Lord is One. Love the Lord your God with all your heart, with all your soul and with all your strength. These words that I am giving you today are to be in your heart. Repeat them to your children. Talk about them when you sit in your house and when you walk along the road, and when you lie down and when you get up."

–Deuteronomy 6:4-7

Any set of biblical foundations for student ministry must include those who have been given the primary responsibility for the spiritual development of teenagers: parents. God has given us two institutions that focus on spiritual development: the home and the church, but He created the home as the principal crucible where spiritual instruction is to occur.

These verses from Deuteronomy point to this fact by instructing parents to hide these teachings in their hearts and then, as they live their lives, to repeat them to their children. It is a picture of parents both telling and living a faithful example in front of their children. It is a demonstration of the declarations of the Shema that our God is one and that we are to love Him with all our heart, soul, and strength.

Following this admonition has serious implications for those of us in student ministry. If this is true, it seems that we should direct a good amount of our ministry focus on strengthening families by partnering with parents in the spiritual development of their students. Practical attention is given to these efforts in chapter 4.

There's also the reality that many parents are uninvolved in church and neglect to teach their teens spiritual truth. While this is true, it does not change the fact that they have been given this responsibility. The solution is for the church to reach out to these parents and introduce them to Christ, reclaim those who have wandered from their faith, and encourage and equip them for this important role. Student ministry belongs to the church, it shouldn't be a satellite ministry in its own orbit. If this is true, we need to muster all the forces available across the church family to join us in reaching uninvolved parents.

Conclusion

Earlier in my life, I (Scott) worked in the construction business for a few years. I was always amazed at the building process and particularly impressed with some of the work I saw on skyscrapers. No matter the size of the project, the first item of business is to set the foundation.

When it comes to laying out a process for student spiritual development, the need is the same. There must be spiritual anchors to serve as the foundation. Ours are based on the bedrock of Scripture:

1. The Great Confession (Matthew 16:13-16)
2. The Great Commandment (Matthew 22:35-40)
3. The Great Commission (Matthew 28:18-20)
4. Jesus' Development (Luke 2:52)
5. The Sermon on the Mount (Matthew 5–7)
6. The Role of Parents (Deuteronomy 6:4-7)

Now we're ready to build an effective strategy for student spiritual development.

CHAPTER 2

THE KNOWN STRATEGY

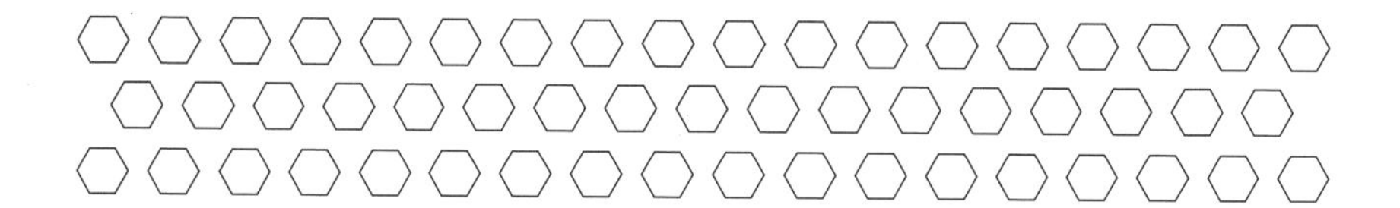

A FRIEND OF MINE (Jeff) once said, “Where there is no strategy, there is no victory.” He was a national and world champion, as well as a bronze medalist in the Olympics. He knew what it took to achieve victory in the sport of wrestling. He would begin with his goal in mind and work backward to determine what he needed to do to achieve his goal. If it meant getting up at five o’clock in the morning to run, working out twice a day, and hitting the sauna at night, that’s what he would do. He knew that he could not just show up, go through the motions, and enjoy victory. He had to have a strategy that would lead him to his goals.

Why would we look at student ministry any differently? Can we really just show up and expect to enjoy the victory of seeing students graduate from our ministries with a passion for Christ and a desire to serve their communities? Can we really just go through the motions of repetitive programming and expect students to remain committed to the local church while they struggle through their young adult life? I don't think any of us intentionally show up at church and expect things to just happen. Most of us do put forth our best effort. But a lot of student ministry across the country, and even the world, is lacking any kind of strategy that would lead to the victories we all want to see in the lives of young people.

Let's look at the elements that define a good strategy.

Elements of a Good Strategy

1. A good strategy will lead you to your defined mark of success.

What kind of success are you chasing after?

For my wrestler friend, it was to become the best wrestler in the world. For you, it may be to become the greatest student minister in your state . . . or to have the largest student ministry in your association . . . or to provide a ministry that leads to the spiritual development of students. Whatever your goal or your mark of success is, a good strategy must lead you there.

2. A good strategy will create a process by which spiritual development occurs.

Movement shows development. If you want to operate with a strategy that leads to the spiritual development of students, your strategy will have to become a road map for the journey. Just as a good road map will always take us from point A to point B, a good strategy for spiritual development will take us from point A (a beginning point in the spiritual development process) to point B (a more mature point in the process).

3. A good strategy will dictate the organizational structure of your student ministry.

The true litmus test for a good strategy is whether or not it affects what we do on a daily basis. Some strategies for student ministry look good in print (and even better in a multimedia presentation), but they never get to the point of affecting the organizational structure of their student ministry. Nothing really changes, which means the student ministry gets the same meager results.

Formulating a Strategy

Most important, a strategy for spiritual development needs to be biblical! At the risk of repetition, let me remind you of the biblical foundation laid out in chapter 1. There are two keys passages we considered:

And Jesus increased in wisdom and stature, and in favor with God and with people.

–Luke 2:52

There was a developmental process in the life of Jesus, and He grew in three ways:

- Wisdom and stature
- Favor with God
- Favor with people

Love the Lord your God with all your heart, with all your soul, and with all your mind. This is the greatest and most important commandment. The second is like it: Love your neighbor as yourself.

–Matthew 22:37-39

We were created for relationships, and Jesus highlighted three distinct relationships in which we are to express love. Look at how these three distinct relationships dovetail perfectly with the three areas that Jesus developed in.

Relationship	**Area of development**
Love for God	Jesus grew in favor with God
Love for ourself	Jesus grew in wisdom and stature
Love for others	Jesus grew in favor with people

Based on Jesus' life and teachings, then, a strategy for spiritual development focuses on how we respond to God, how we see ourselves in light of God, and how we treat others in light of what Christ has done for us. We have pulled this together in what we call the KNOWN strategy. Spiritual development happens as we help students KNOW God, OWN their faith, and make their faith KNOWN.

KNOW

The first pillar of spiritual growth is upward development: KNOWing God. Just as Jesus increased in favor with God, so can students. We want to make sure students understand and know who God is—not just what God will do for them, but who He is. What does the Scripture tell us about His character and His nature? As students begin to understand the basics of God's character and nature, they better understand His response to them through His Son and, in turn, their response to Him.

OWN

The second pillar of spiritual growth is inward development: students learning to OWN their faith. Just as Jesus increased in wisdom and stature and taught us that we are to love others as we love ourselves, we want students to take ownership of their faith and who they are in Christ.

We're not always comfortable with talk about loving ourselves. We have been taught for years that there is nothing good about us and, in our sinful nature, we are deserving of hell and damnation for all of eternity. While I (Jeff) believe in the depravity of man and the eternal destination of the nonbeliever, I refuse to believe that we maintain that identity after conversion. Just as we must teach students that they are depraved in their sinful nature, we must also teach them that once they come to Christ, they are redeemed children of the King! We are not what we used to be; we are what Jesus Christ has declared about us. We are not promoting an ego trip; rather we are encouraging an identity in Christ based on what Scripture states about us. It is not self esteem, it is Christ esteem!

Too many students are looking to the world to validate their existence and provide their identity. Students go through struggles while trying to find purpose in their lives and trying to answer simple questions like: How did I get here? Why am I here? As they walk through those struggles, they need to know—and own—what Jesus Christ has said about them.

When my own teenagers wake up in the morning and look at themselves in the mirror, I do not want them to see a teenager struggling to be accepted at their school or struggling to be accepted in their community. I want them to see a child of the King. I want them to see a son or daughter of Christ. I want them to know that they are a part of this royal priesthood that Scripture talks about.

As students learn to own their faith, they will grasp their true identity and be prepared to face a world that would love to define for them both who they are and why they are here.

KNOWN

The third pillar of spiritual growth is outward development: students learning to make their faith KNOWN.

Just as Jesus increased in favor with people and taught us to love our neighbors, students can do the same. And as they do so, they make their faith KNOWN.

Let us offer a side note here: There is a reciprocal relationship between OWNing your faith and making your faith KNOWN. In other words, how you respond to your neighbor is in direct proportion to how you see yourself. How did Jesus say you are to love your neighbor? As yourself. But what if you do not like yourself? What if you do not have a Christ identity and are not grounded in a Christ-centered esteem? Jesus said that we will respond to the needs of our neighbors based on how we understand and own who we are in Him. We cannot encourage students to make their faith KNOWN without also leading them to KNOW God and OWN their faith.

Jesus spoke on several occasions about trees and their fruit (Matt. 7:15-23; John 15:1-8), passages that shed light on what it looks like for believers to make their faith KNOWN. Ever seen an apple farmer standing in front of his orchard convincing his trees that they have to bear fruit? No, farmers cultivate their orchards and make sure that their trees are healthy. What happens? Trees bear fruit. They produce fruit because of what they are.

When students understand who God is, and when they believe and own what God has said about them, there will be a natural process by which spiritual fruit is produced. They will naturally make their faith KNOWN. Spiritually healthy students produce spiritual fruit—fruit that will last for eternity. As we emphasize this concept of outward development we will see a transformation in students' attitude toward loving their neighbor and a great harvest of fruit produced for the King.

Core Competencies

In the previous chapter, we saw how the Sermon on the Mount describes six core competencies that are needed for spiritual development. Let's review:

Matthew 5:1-12	Character
Matthew 5:13-20	Influence
Matthew 5:21-48	Relationships
Matthew 6:1-24	Disciplines
Matthew 6:25-34	Lordship
Matthew 7:1-27	Discernment

Consider these six areas of competency in light of the three pillars for spiritual growth.

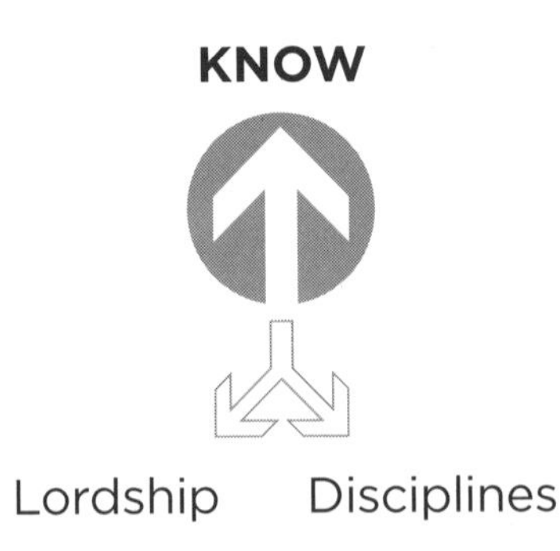

We want students to KNOW God. We help them do that as we teach them about the nature and character of God and who Jesus is—all issues of lordship. Once they have surrendered to Jesus as Lord and Savior, they grow in their knowledge of Him as they practice a variety of disciplines, including prayer, Bible study, giving, and so forth.

OWN

Character Discernment

We want students to OWN their faith. We do this as we help them see themselves as Christ sees them and develop Christlike character. Teaching them to make wise choices (discernment) is an important part of taking ownership of what they believe.

KNOWN

Relationships Influence

We want students to make their faith KNOWN. They do that through their relationships and the influence they have in those relationships including: family, friends, the church, and the world.

The KNOWN strategy is simple, straightforward, and biblical. There is one other factor we need to add: the primary settings where this strategy is taught and modeled.

Home and Church

God has given us two institutions where spiritual development is taught and nurtured: the home and the church. We usually think of student ministry in the context of the church (or a parachurch group), but we need a new perspective. The home plays a critical role.

We've mentioned the importance of Luke 2:52, but we also need to remember the preceding verse.

Then he went down to Nazareth with them and was obedient to them. But his mother treasured all these things in her heart.

–Luke 2:51

Jesus understood the importance and value of His earthly mom and dad. He submitted Himself to their authority.

As student ministers, we need to lift up moms and dads or guardians as the primary spiritual developer for students. We don't want to assume that responsibility. The truth is we *can't* assume that responsibility. Even in homes where the parents are poor role models, they are still the key influencers in their children's lives.

So what is our responsibility as student leaders? We are to partner with moms and dads in this process of spiritual development. We can become one of many partners who aid moms and dads in that process. We truly believe that parents want to serve in that role, but most of them do not understand what that means. So we become their partners.

- We champion them in their role as the primary spiritual developers.
- We train them.
- We resource them
- We encourage them.
- We involve them in ministry.

We become *secondary* spiritual developers.

But I have students whose parents aren't involved or interested! What happens to their kids? God still works through those of us in this secondary role! We are going to dig into this in chapter 4 as we look at practical ways to help parents become KNOWN parents.

One thing we can assure you is that the vast majority, if not all, parents and guardians love their teenagers. As a student minister, you love those same students. You share something in common! Take advantage of that common denominator. By helping parents understand and live out their role, you are definitely influencing the teenagers you care about.

Let us ask the question again: Are you providing a balanced approach to student spiritual development through your ministry? We cannot determine the choices that a student will make. What we can determine is what type of ministry we will provide and where it will lead students. Let's make it our goal and strategy—our battle cry—to help students KNOW God, OWN their faith, and make their faith KNOWN.

CHAPTER 3

DEVELOPING KNOWN STUDENTS

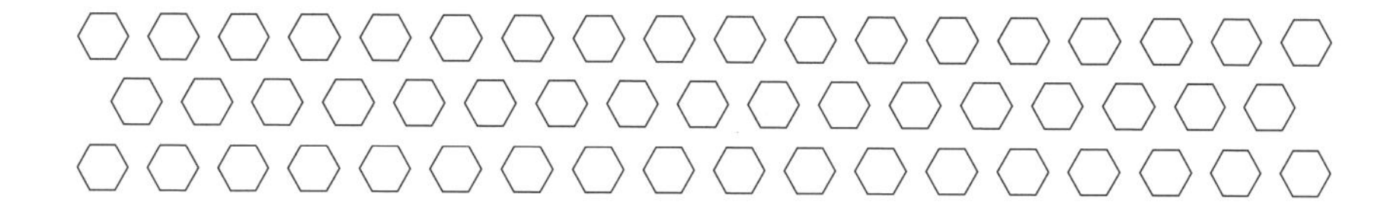

BEGIN WITH THE END IN MIND. Are you familiar with this maxim? I (Scott) think it is particularly valuable related to travel—especially if you are doing the driving. Last summer, in preparation for a mission trip to Philadelphia with some of my church's high school students, I purchased a GPS. I love it, and I want you to know that I came to trust and respect Samantha (that is the name by which we refer to my GPS), especially as we traveled the crowded streets of inner-city Philly each day.

But, Samantha helped us the most on our way back to Nashville. I had thought we would take a similar return route back through Delaware, Baltimore, D.C., and so on, but Samantha had a different idea. After proving her trustworthiness in Philadelphia, I was game for a travel adventure, and since I was leading our group, our other van had to follow as well. Samantha led us west out of Philadelphia. By doing so we were able to enjoy unencumbered interstate all the way to Tennessee, bypassing the congestion of the D.C. corridor. In fact, we saved a night in a hotel by carving about four hours off our trip!

When it comes to our ministry with students, just like Samantha, we need to begin with the end in mind. Where are we headed? What sort of outcomes do we want to see in the lives of our students as they navigate their spiritual journey? Can we serve as a sort of "spiritual GPS," helping to guide them in their spiritual development? What skills do you desire for your students as they prepare to graduate from high school and step into the rest of their lives?

We've already discussed the biblical foundations for student ministry and laid out a strategy for student spiritual development. Let's spend a little more time with the core competencies we identified in the previous chapter. This information will lay the groundwork for all that follows: partnering with parents and choosing curriculum, camps, events, service projects, leadership development programs, and other student ministry resources that will best meet the needs of the teenagers in our circle of influence.

Signs of Progress

Just like the road signs that let us know we are getting closer to our destination, or even GPS devices that compute our anticipated time of arrival, there are some spiritual markers of progress for students. We have identified them as core competencies: the desired outcomes (goals and indicators) related to the KNOWN strategy for student spiritual development.

KNOW GOD

SIGN OF PROGRESS 1: Students will KNOW Christ as they submit to His lordship and practice spiritual disciplines.

☐ **GOAL FOR LORDSHIP:** Students will recognize and respond to the lordship of Christ.

Both the beginning point and ultimate destination for our students is the recognition of their need for a Savior and their ongoing surrender to His desires for their lives.

▶ **INDICATORS:**

1. Experience personal salvation.—Every teenager needs to know Jesus Christ. One way we can help is by simply giving students the opportunity to hear and respond to the gospel. Let's not make the assumption that all of our students have already made this decision. It is also important to explain to students that this commitment is a personal decision—not one their parents or other well-meaning adults or friends can make for them. People are *born* one at a time and *reborn* one at a time.

2. Walk with assurance of their salvation.—After making a decision for Christ, students need immediate follow-up to help them grow in their relationship with the Lord and to gain an assurance of their salvation. It has been said that to lead someone to Christ and then not disciple him or her is spiritual child abuse. Some teens may not have much experience with long-term relationships, and they need to know the God who saved them will not desert them. Honest doubts need to be addressed through Scripture and the counsel of a mature believer.

3. Order their lives based on the lordship of Christ.—Setting priorities in life is important, and yet being willing to submit our desires to the lordship of Christ is a constant struggle. Since students are in a stage of life in which they are developing habits, it is a great season to begin practicing submission to Christ. Students need both instruction and encouragement in the area of lordship and a taste of the blessings that such obedience can bring. There are a lot of voices trying to persuade teens as they set priorities. They need opportunities to hear directly from the One who cares for them most.

4. Exhibit an understanding of each member of the Trinity.—It sounds like a pretty challenging goal, huh? The idea is that students will gain a balanced understanding of the Father, Son, and Holy Spirit. It can be tempting to focus on the life of Christ and the teachings of the New Testament, but students also need a comprehensive view of God the Father, and exposure to the full counsel of God's Word. In addition, sometimes we speak so little about the person of the Holy Spirit, it makes you wonder if we are afraid He might show up!

5. Seek God's will in daily decisions.—Every moment students are faced with decisions, and each choice will be based on someone's will. It's amazing how seeking God's will in even the small decisions of life can positively impact teens. It's natural for us to consider our own desires first, and society will applaud us for doing so. But students can be encouraged to be countercultural, to actively seek God in their daily choices.

6. Resist temptation in the power of Christ.—Students *can* resist the temptations they face, though many teens believe they are powerless to do so. In reality, they are powerless on their own, but through the strength of a vital, committed relationship with Jesus Christ, they can plug into the power needed to resist temptation. Remember Jesus' experience with the Devil in the wilderness? We must equip students for the spiritual war they are in, beginning with the only offensive weapon in the armor of God—the sword of the Spirit, the Word of God.

☐ **GOAL FOR DISCIPLINES:** Students will practice spiritual disciplines.

Teens are capable of developing spiritual habits that can become lifelong disciplines and propel them to greater intimacy in their relationship with Jesus.

▶ INDICATORS

1. Develop a lifestyle of daily prayer.—Students need to experience the benefits of an ongoing conversation with God, as well as concentrated times of fervent prayer. In tandem with placing this goal before teens, we must also show them how to pray by providing resources and demonstrating examples of a variety of ways to experience prayer. The Bible contains numerous examples of prayer. We should remember the goal is increased intimacy with the Lord. Human relationships are built on communication. It is the same in our relationship with God.

2. Develop the habit of daily Bible reading, meditation, and Scripture memory.—If we can inspire students to treasure God's Word, we will have an accomplishment worth celebrating. They need to see Scripture as a valuable gift and guide. We need to demonstrate its relevance to their lives so they can come to understand that it is more than a history book; it is what it claims to be—the living Word of God. Once valued in such a manner, crossing the bridge to meditating on it and hiding it in their hearts will become much easier.

3. Develop a lifestyle of worship.—We must stretch the parameters of our students' understanding of worship. Worship is our response to a loving God. It includes a variety of musical expressions, but at its heart is so much more than music alone. Helping students value the Object of our worship over a particular style of worship is a step in the right direction. Then we can move to the weightier issues of what it means to be a living sacrifice and how everything we say and do can be an offering of worship.

4. Identify and utilize their spiritual gifts.—One of the greatest needs for student ministry leaders and parents is to help students discover their spiritual gifts, and then to create opportunities for teens to exercise these gifts. Today's students are wonderfully gifted and have a diverse array of skills that can benefit the cause of Christ. We fall short when all we provide is a spiritual gifts inventory to our students. Concrete avenues of involvement in the church must accompany these diagnostic tools. This strategy can reduce the number of students dropping out of the church.

5. Manage the resources God has given them.—Wouldn't it be great if students (and adults) understood the difference between *ownership* and *stewardship*? God has called us all to be stewards of the things He has given us. He is the owner, and we are the managers. These resources include time, talents, possessions, and relationships. As Jesus explained in the Sermon on the Mount, our attitudes and the condition of our hearts determine our behavior and our view of the purpose and use of our resources. Students can truly get ahead of the game by understanding and practicing the concept of stewardship.

6. Live consistently by faith in God.—Students are natural risk takers, well-known for their willingness to push the envelope to experience the thrill of danger. We need to tap into this tendency and present them with a daring proposition for their lives—to live consistently by faith in God. This challenge, if accepted, could lead to an army of Christ-followers willing to live out their faith regardless of the consequences. It boils down to a matter of trust. Are we willing to demonstrate our ultimate faith in God so we can provide an example for students to follow? Even when we can't see His hand, will we trust His heart?

OWN YOUR FAITH

SIGN OF PROGRESS 2: Students will OWN their faith as they grow in character and discernment.

☐ **GOAL FOR CHARACTER:** Students will develop and demonstrate Christ's character.

True ownership of our faith is dependent on seeking to conform our character to the character of Christ. As students take on the mind of Christ, He will shape their attitudes, words, and actions.

▶ INDICATORS

1. Seek to honor God through a lifestyle of holiness.—Students need an understanding of what it means to be holy—to be set apart for God—in their daily lives. They need to know that holiness is not being "odd for God" but consists of lifestyle choices that are more focused on saying "yes" to the things of God, to things of eternal value. This obedience is difficult when it is so tempting to be influenced by selfish motives, and drawn to self-serving choices, and pressured by others. Students need living examples of holiness and affirmation of their right choices.

2. *Consistently display the fruit of the Spirit.*—Love, joy, peace, patience, kindness, goodness, faith, gentleness, and self-control—what a list! Just think what our youth groups and our churches would be like if every Christian consistently displayed the fruit of the Spirit. Why it might even make church business meetings pleasant! There's only one catch—for the fruit to be evident, the Spirit must be in control. So the pivotal question is not, how much of the Holy Spirit do I have? but rather, how much of me does the Holy Spirit have?

3. *Display honesty, integrity, and purity.*—It seems like these three character qualities are less and less common. One of my favorite questions for Christian students centers on cheating in school. While the overwhelming majority will agree with me that cheating is wrong (usually after a long discussion about homework vs. tests), this same majority will admit to practicing this very behavior. Students must see that while choosing honesty, integrity, and purity can be costly to them in the short run, displaying these character traits will ultimately be beneficial to them and to their future endeavors.

4. *Strive for excellence in all aspects of life.*—It is incredible to see the amount of time, effort, and money students will invest in the things that are important to them. Everything from band to football to cheerleading to the debate team to a drama performance to preparing for college entrance exams will be approached with a relentless commitment to excellence. This dedication is wonderful, for we believe we honor God when we do our very best with the gifts and abilities He has given us. Just one more thought, shouldn't we also strive for such excellence in our relationship with Him?

5. Develop a self-image based on who they are in Christ.—Students need a biblical understanding of their worth. Scripture states that we are all "remarkably and wonderfully made" (Ps. 139), but often students do not feel this way. Comparing themselves to the images they see online, on TV, in the movies, in magazines, or even in the hallways at school can leave them feeling less than confident about their identity. Let's point them to God's truth and back that up by affirming their worth through our words and actions.

6. Develop the heart of a servant.—An essential element of Christ's character is how He embodied servanthood. While teenagers are notorious for being self-absorbed, they also have a great capacity for serving others. They need the opportunity to experience the reward of helping someone and the powerful realization that they can be used by God in the work of His kingdom. Such experiences can chart the course for a lifetime of faithful service. And just a reminder, today's students will be tomorrow's leaders—both inside and outside the church.

☐ **GOAL FOR DISCERNMENT:** Students will make wise decisions.

As students grow, so does the complexity and weight of the decisions they make. These decisions can have tremendous impact on the rest of their lives. Acquiring godly wisdom and being able to apply it in practical ways are crucial.

▶ **INDICATORS:**

1. Affirm Scripture as the authoritative guide for their lives.—One of the interesting things about teens is their ability to affirm any number of philosophies simultaneously—even if some ideas appear to be contradictory. For some students, this tendency can lead to a do-it-yourself, custom-designed belief system—taking bits and pieces from any number of spiritual ideas and forming their own version. We can't assume they know of the guidance the Bible offers for their lives or why they should trust it. They need information on the veracity and reliability of the Bible and an understanding of how the God who created them has provided a road map for life.

2. Apply Scriptural principles to daily decisions.—Can you remember a point in your life when the Bible began to read more like a newspaper than a history book? when it seemed like the realities of your life were being revealed in Scripture? Students need these encounters so they can realize that God's Word really is living and active. It is one thing for us to provide Scriptural guidance for students by answering their questions about daily decisions, but it is quite another to equip them to search the Bible for themselves. Such practice can build confidence in teens as they make decisions that honor God.

3. Assume responsibility for their decisions.—One of the key ingredients in students OWNing their faith is assuming responsibility for their decisions. This accountability can be a tough hurdle, and oftentimes well-meaning parents and student ministry leaders contribute to the challenge. Frequently teens do not get the chance to experience the consequences of their decisions because an adult steps in to lessen their impact. Students are capable of more than we sometimes give them credit for—including the ability to be accountable for the choices they make.

4. *Recognize true teaching from false teaching.*—In a world overflowing with information and various forms of media that are powerful and persuasive tools, how does a teenager decide what is true and what is false? For that matter, how do they know if the person promoting a certain point of view today will not be revealed as a fraud tomorrow? Unfortunately, many of us like being told what we are to think and believe, and we choose not to give critical consideration to the information we consume. Teens must be armed with the ability to view any teaching they receive through the filter of Scripture. Much like recognizing counterfeit currency, they need to become so familiar with the heart, nature, and truth of God that anything contrary to Him will be easily recognized.

5. *Possess and articulate a biblical worldview.*—It is critical for students to have a comprehensive view of who God is, who they are, and why they are in the world. A biblical worldview helps to ground them in their identity and provides a framework for understanding God's purpose for their lives. Possessing such a Christian worldview is the foundation, but teens also need instruction and practice in Christian apologetics so they can explain and defend their worldview to others. The ability to do so can increase their confidence when opportunities arise to share their faith.

6. *Recognize and avoid the negative aspects of peer pressure.*—Peer approval is a strong motivating force in the lives of students (and even in the lives of adults). It hits us at our basic desire for acceptance and a sense of belonging. One of the keys to avoiding bad decisions is the recognition of circumstances that can lead to poor

decision making. This is where we need to start with students—helping them recognize people and situations that can lead to compromise. Once dangerous conditions are identified, teens must be ready to locate the way of escape and take it.

MAKE YOUR FAITH KNOWN

SIGN OF PROGRESS 3: Students will make their faith KNOWN as they develop in relationships and influence.

☐ **GOAL FOR RELATIONSHIPS:** Students will develop godly relationships.

Spiritual development does not occur in a vacuum but in the crucible of relationships. God created us for relationships, and teens need to know how to have healthy interactions with others.

▶ **INDICATORS:**

1. Recognize and submit to proper authorities.—This task can be a tricky one for adolescents. Just as they are reaching for more independence, they are faced with the responsibility of submitting to authorities. The realization that parents, teachers, coaches, bosses, and even governmental authorities are not infallible can make submission increasingly difficult. We must aid students in understanding that submitting to proper authorities is ultimately an expression of obedience to God.

2. Encourage and minister to fellow believers of all ages.—Too often churches provide ministry *to* students instead of ministry *with* students. Teenagers are equal members in the body of Christ and can utilize their gifts, abilities, and talents to build up the church. This service includes crossing generational lines to minister to fellow believers. Few churches can pull off Vacation Bible School without the help of their teenagers. In addition, students can encourage senior saints in their church with acts of kindness and service. This is what a church family is all about.

3. Cultivate relationships with non-Christians.—How do we help students be *in* the world and not *of* the world? Teens are most effective at reaching their peers for Christ, but these opportunities won't happen if they're not cultivating relationships with non-Christians. If students are going to be on God's mission in the world, we cannot shield them from contact with those who have yet to surrender to Christ. Jesus is once again the example we need to follow. He was able to relate to all kinds of people—sinners and saints—yet He spent the majority of His time with a small group of like-minded followers. Students need guidance in reaching the proper balance in their relationships. What if churches and student ministries were viewed as launching pads into the world rather than sanctuaries of seclusion?

4. Support their families by loving them and acting responsibly.—One of the hardest places to live out the Christian faith can be the home. It is the place where our family members know all of our faults and shortcomings, but it can also be a place where selfless love and service can be modeled and encouraged. It's healthy for students to realize that their choices—whether positive or negative—also affect their families. Sometimes teens may need to take the lead in showing love and forgiveness to parents and siblings. They can choose to demonstrate love through their words and actions. In so doing, they set positive patterns for their future families.

5. Strengthen and encourage their friends.—Few things are more important to teenagers than their friends. Students who are moving to an ownership of their faith can be proactive in ministering to their friends. Listening, encouraging, affirming, holding friends accountable, and showing unconditional love are examples of the love of Christ. The Bible tells us God reconciled Himself to the world through Christ and that we have been given this ministry of reconciliation. One of the best places to start this ministry is with our friends.

6. Deal with conflict in a Christlike manner.—Conflict, in and of itself, is not a sin. Where we can get into trouble is in how we deal with conflict. (Which reminds me of why I [Scott] don't have a fish on my car—I would hate to embarrass the church!) It's essential for students to understand that conflict is normal, but we must also equip them with the skills to handle conflict in a Christlike manner. It seems like we've lost a little civility in this area and that it is more difficult than ever to disagree in an agreeable manner. We need to help our students know how to approach a variety of conflicts in ways that will honor Christ.

☐ **GOAL FOR INFLUENCE:** Students will make an intentional impact on others.

Seeking to influence outside the context of relationship is a dead end. God wants to use students to impact their world as they live out their faith in intentional ways.

▶ INDICATORS

1. Actively participate in the life and ministry of the local church.—What is your church's view of teenagers? Are they seen only as the church of tomorrow or are they viewed as full-fledged members who are willing and able to make a contribution to kingdom work today? Achieving the best results will require both the church and the student ministry to step out of their comfort zones. Much has been written about the problems with the "one-eared Mickey Mouse" model of youth ministry (a small circle or group that is barely connected to the larger circle, the rest of the church). Churches need to take advantage of students' enthusiasm and creativity. And make no mistake, students also have the responsibility of choosing to jump in and participate in the ministries of their church even when doing so requires them to step out of their comfort zones.

2. Lead someone to faith in Christ.—One of the most significant events in the life of a young Christian is the moment they lead someone to faith in Christ. Pushing past potential fear to share their faith and seeing God use them in His redemptive plan is an amazing experience. Seeing the power of God displayed in a way that changes someone for eternity can motivate students toward a lifestyle of witnessing. Students need to know they are an integral part of God's plan to reach a lost planet.

3. Participate in mission and ministry projects.—Students are willing to invest their hearts and lives into causes they believe will make a difference in the world. Through involvement in mission and ministry projects, students have opportunities to live out their faith in practical ways. There is also great value when these projects are student-initiated and student-led. While teens need coaching and encouragement as their faith develops, we should never do something for them that we could lead them to do themselves.

4. Confront the culture with the love of Christ.—God has called His followers to be agents of change in the world. Can you envision teenagers who are willing to confront the accepted norms found in our culture? I am convinced they can do it, but the key will be to do so with the love of Christ. Let's encourage our students to be salt and light in an ever-darkening world instead of allowing them to become complaining cynics. Students have the capacity both to speak and live out the truth in love.

5. Defend their faith and beliefs.—It's one thing for teens to make positive choices, it is another for them to be able to communicate why they made the positive choice. In a world filled with diverse faiths, it is not enough for students to adhere to a Christian system of beliefs. They need training and practice in defending their faith. Their home and church should be ideal places for such preparation to take place. Students need exposure to other belief systems and guidance to understand the major tenets of other religions and how they differ from Christianity.

6. *Use their abilities and talents in evangelism.*—As mentioned earlier, students are incredibly gifted, and the ultimate goal should be for them to use their abilities and talents to advance the gospel. Examples include using the Internet and social media as evangelism tools; creating music, videos, and other artistic expression; and leading campus-related outreach projects. The church and youth group can serve as incubators for teens to develop their gifts and to experiment and refine them for greater effectiveness.

Using the Goals and Indicators

We've just taken a look at 36 indicators that are descriptive of students who are moving forward in their spiritual development by coming to KNOW Christ, OWN their faith, and make their faith KNOWN. These indicators are not occurring in a linear fashion but are as multidimensional and unique as each student God has created. One way to use these indicators is to survey the students, parents, and student ministry leaders of your church about the relative presences of each of these indicators. This evaluation will provide a snapshot of the perceptions observed by each of these groups. The results can then be used to guide purposeful choices related to events, themes, curriculum, training, and so forth to be used in your student ministry. A sample survey has been provided in Appendix 1 ("Building KNOWN Students Survey," p. 119). Use the results to help you form your plan for developing students through your student ministry. This survey could be easily adapted for use with leaders and parents.

CHAPTER 4

DEVELOPING KNOWN PARENTS

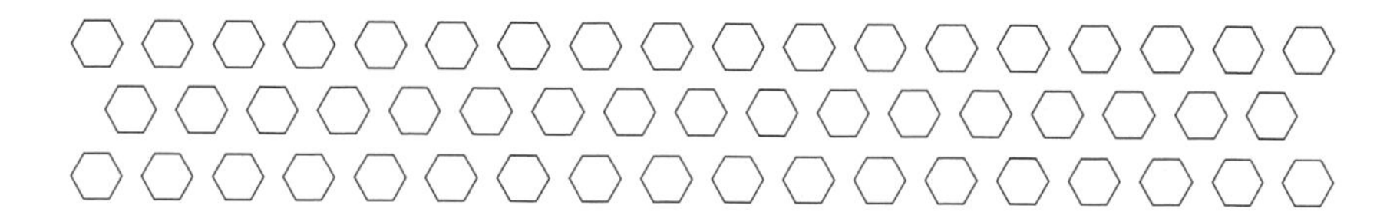

PARENTS DO NOT HAVE enough time in the day. They run from one practice to the next, hoping their kids will not miss anything. Can they cover all the bases and provide a balanced approach to life for their kids?

Parents need a partner. They may be the primary spiritual developers of their kids, but they need like-minded adults who will walk alongside them and provide development opportunities for their students.

Thank God for teachers who will walk alongside them in the *educational* development of their students. Thank God for coaches who will walk alongside them in the *physical* development of their students. But what about the *spiritual* development of their students?

In 2007, LifeWay Research conducted a study into the church dropout problem. This study looked at the number of students who drop out of church after they leave high school. There were some pretty alarming findings in the study, but perhaps the most important concerned the role of parents. (You can find more information on the "Church Dropout Study" at *www.lifewayresearch.com,* look under the "Previous Studies" tab.)

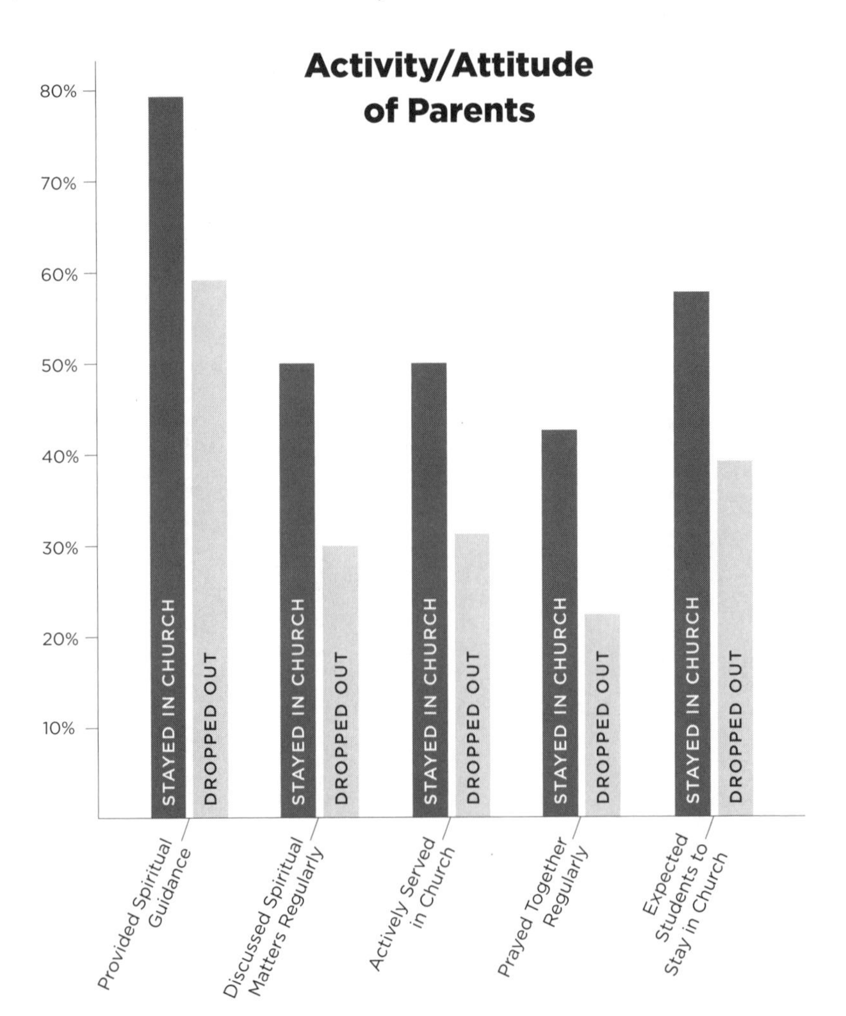

Spiritual guidance.—One factor that contributed to a higher percentage of dropouts among students after high school was a lack of spiritual guidance. Research showed that 79 percent of the students who stayed in church said their parents provided some form of spiritual guidance, compared to only 59 percent of the students who dropped out of church.

Spiritual discussions.—Research revealed that 50 percent of the students who stayed involved in church said their parents discussed spiritual matters with them regularly, while only 30 percent of the dropouts said their parents discussed spiritual matters with them.

Church involvement.—Parents' church involvement also played a role. The same 50 percent of students who stayed in church said their parents actively served in the church, while only 31 percent of the dropouts said their parents served in the church.

Prayer.—Research revealed that 42 percent of students who stayed in church said their parents prayed with them regularly, while only 22 percent of the dropouts had parents who prayed with them.

Expectations.—This study also reported that 57 percent of students who stayed in church said their parents expressed an expectation that they would remain in church after the age of 17, while only 39 percent of dropouts said their parents expressed the same expectation.

Parents make a difference!

The Parent Partnership

Parents desperately need student ministers to partner with them in the spiritual development of their students.

In this strategic partnership, the parents and the student minister work *together* to provide an environment that offers teenagers the best opportunity to grow spiritually. Even the best parents in the world need a partner in this difficult task.

This partnership is established with a single goal in mind: the spiritual development of the student. What happens in the home needs to connect with what is happening in the church and vice versa!

Consider the Parent Partnership as a way to connect you with parents and assist them in the process of student spiritual development. The Parent Partnership can give purpose to your ministry and drive your plans for student spiritual formation. (See Appendix 4, "The Parent Partnership," p. 127.)

A Vision for the Partnership

Parents and student ministers can agree on what they are working toward: spiritually-developed teenagers who remain connected to the body of Christ through their college years and beyond; students who allow their faith to guide them as they make life-changing choices. Work with parents to create a vision statement that reflects this common goal for their students.

As you develop your vision statement keep it short, precise, measurable, and attainable. This statement will drive the rest of the process, so make sure it is leading to the spiritual destination where parents want their students to arrive.

Here is a sample vision statement:

A Vision for Student Spiritual Development

When _______________ graduates from high school, he/she will be able to:

- Recognize and respond to the lordship of Christ.
- Express his/her faith through the practice of spiritual disciplines.
- Develop and demonstrate Christ's character in his/her life.
- Make wise decisions.
- Develop and maintain godly relationships.
- Intentionally and positively impact the lives of others.

What parent would not want these outcomes in their teenager's life? This can happen if we will become more strategic in our approach to student spiritual development as we partner with parents. So how do we carry out this vision statement?

The answer is in the previous chapter on developing KNOWN students. The goals and indicators outlined there are not just actions for the student leader. Let's consider ways you can support parents in *their* work toward these goals.

1. Lordship.—As you talk with parents about recognizing and responding to the lordship of Christ, share your desire to see their student experience personal salvation and be able to walk in assurance of that salvation. Obviously, we can't force that to happen, but we can do things in both the home and church to create opportunities for students to respond to Christ. Once salvation is experienced, the desire is that students will begin to understand how to order their lives based on the lordship of Christ.

2. Spiritual Disciplines.—Parents can model and encourage the practices of prayer, daily Bible reading, and giving—just to name a few. These disciplines will allow students to grow in their understanding of who God is, as well as experience His grace in their lives.

3. Character.—Developing and demonstrating Christ's character in students lives deals more with who they are becoming and not what they are doing. Parents can be encouraged to model Christlike character. Work with parents to understand and teach traits like purity, honesty, integrity, and the pursuit of excellence.

4. Discernment.—Making wise decisions is always important to parents, because they know that teenagers do not always make the best decisions! Work with parents to develop teenagers who understand and apply biblical principles to the decisions of everyday life.

5. Relationships.—Developing relationships comes easily to most teenagers, but what about healthy relationships? Parents want their teenagers to avoid destructive relationships, and we can partner with them to teach the value of godly relationships.

6. Influence.—We can help parents model and train their teenagers to live lives of godly influence on those around them. Our teenagers have a great opportunity to help shape and mold lives, so we partner with parents to help them understand their responsibility to influence others for Christ.

The Strategy for the Partnership

What is going to happen to ensure that a proposed partnership focused on spiritual development becomes a reality? The KNOWN strategy—the strategy that drives your student ministry—is the same one that drives your Parent Partnership.

Most parents do not approach parenting strategically. It's done on the move—putting out the next fire or dealing with the next crisis. What an incredible blessing it would be for parents to know they are on a purposeful path that is strategic in leading their students to spiritual development.

The KNOWN strategy for student spiritual development is also a strategy for the home. Our goal in this partnership is to see a connection between the home and the church. Introduce parents—whether in a group setting or individually—to the KNOWN strategy. Begin by reviewing the biblical foundation presented in chapter 1:

1. Developmental foundation—Luke 2:52. (See pp. 26-30.)
2. Relational foundation—Matthew 22:37-38. (See pp. 20-23.)
3. Core competency foundation—Matthew 5–7. (See pp. 30-32.)

Explain to parents the three major areas of spiritual development presented in chapter 2 (pp. 39-42).

Finally, help parents discover how they can help their students KNOW God, OWN their faith, and make their faith KNOWN by introducing them to the spiritual markers of progress identified in chapter 3.

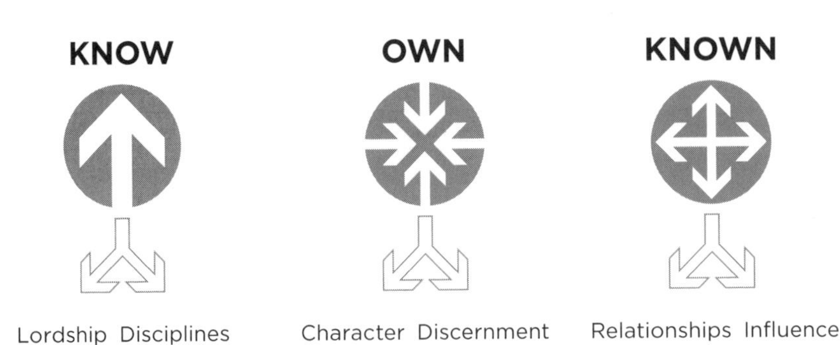

The effectiveness of this strategic approach to spiritual development will be affected by the willingness and desire of both the primary spiritual developer (the parents) and the secondary spiritual developers (the student leaders) to carry out the strategy.

The Parent's Role in the Partnership

Last year I (Jeff) was teaching a class at my church for parents of teenagers. We were having a great discussion on the topic of student spiritual development. I asked the parents if they felt like they were assuming the role of spiritual developer in the lives of their students. Almost every hand in the class went up. I was surprised that so many parents felt like they were doing this, but surprise turned to shock when I asked the next question: How are you fulfilling that role? A parent spoke up and said, "We are bringing them to you!"

While I appreciated their vote of confidence, their idea of leading in the spiritual development of their students was no more than dropping them off at church. They felt that, if they could just get their kids to the religious professional, then everything would work out all right.

Before we roll our eyes at such parental thinking, those of us in church leadership need to evaluate how we might have encouraged this. The church calls age-group specialists and ministers. The church creates and promotes a host of age-appropriate activities, studies, and ministries. We don't merely babysit children and teenagers while parents attend church; we teach and work with their children. All this can be good, provided we are not unintentionally implying that the church and its religious professionals are offering everything the family needs.

Let's lift up and restore the role of the parent. Deuteronomy 6:1-9 paints a clear picture of the role of the parent as the primary spiritual developer in the life of the student:

This is the command—the statutes and ordinances—the Lord your God has instructed me to teach you, so that you may follow them in the land you are about to enter and possess. Do this so that you may fear the Lord your God all the days of your life by keeping all His statutes and commands I am giving you, your son, and your grandson, and so that you may have a long life. Listen, Israel, and be careful to follow them, so that you may prosper and multiply greatly, because the Lord, the God of your fathers, has promised you a land flowing with milk and honey.

Listen, Israel: The Lord *our God, the* Lord *is One. Love the* Lord *your God with all your heart, with all your soul, and with all your strength. These words that I am giving you today are to be in your heart. Repeat them to your children. Talk about them when you sit in your house and when you walk along the road, when you lie down and when you get up. Bind them as a sign on your hand and let them be a symbol on your forehead. Write them on the doorposts of your house and on your gates.*

What is the first responsibility of parents? To love God with all of their heart, soul, and strength. There is nothing more important to the spiritual development of students than for them to see their parents living out their faith. The home becomes the classroom where faith is learned, and it becomes the lab where faith is tested.

Moses called parents to create environments in the home through which spiritual development can occur. The encouragement to write God's statutes and commands "on the doorposts of your house" becomes a blueprint to make sure homes are reflecting the values and principles of Scripture. The encouragement to teach our children "when you lie down and when you get up" becomes a battle cry to make sure parents are taking advantage of every teachable moment. This moves beyond just talking about Jesus during bedtime prayers and blessings at meal times.

Let's consider some practical ways parents can live out Deuteronomy 6.

Prayer.—Encourage parents to create an environment in their homes where spiritual development can occur. One way to do this is simply by praying together. Pray at meals. Pray blessings over their students. Pray together at night before they go to bed. Nighttime prayer can be a group experience, or it can one-on-one. One-on-one prayer allows for different evening schedules, and can be more conducive to private conversations that might accompany the prayer time.

Teachable moments.—Encourage parents to take advantage of opportunities to convey spiritual truth. These are not planned Bible studies, but those opportunities that sneak up on you, those teachable moments. Parents should ask God to give them the spiritual sensitivity to recognize when a teachable moment has dropped into their laps.

Planned discussions.—Picture this: a teenager participates in a Bible study, Sunday School class, or small-group study. Sometime during the next few days, one of his or her parents engages him or her in discussion around the same topic or Scripture. This is not the typical "What did you learn in class today?" question. These are specific questions to engage the student in discussing key truths he or she learned and talking about how those truths apply to everyday life.

Let me stress that this is not a quiz, trying to determine if the teenager was listening in class! You can put many parents at ease by assuring them that they are not teaching (or re-teaching) the lesson. Many parents do not feel qualified to teach or lead a Bible study. Also assure them we are not calling them to answer all their teenager's Bible questions. (Actually, a teenager may be more engaged if the parent doesn't pretend to have all the answers.) We are calling them to a conversation.

All of us are on a spiritual pilgrimage, and we're going down this road together. A teenager can benefit from hearing his or her parent's own struggles on a topic or how the passage had helped him or her in the past.

Encourage parents to initiate these discussions anytime. It doesn't have to be a designated time and place each week. For example, sitting in the car together waiting at the drive-thru can be a great place to start a casual conversation.

"I know on Sunday your class talked about being created in the image of God. How do you see yourself in the image of God?"

How can the parent know what questions to ask? You! As the student leader, you provide questions and/or discussion points related to students' weekly Bible studies. Appendix 2, "Recommended Resources," (p. 122) offers several Bible study resources that provide parent support.

This moves us to the other player in the parent partnership.

The Student Minister's Role in the Partnership

A balanced approach to spiritual development utilizes both the home and the church. Parents have the responsibility for the home, and the student minister assumes responsibility for the church. We need to provide resources for parents and additional opportunities for balanced spiritual development for students.

Student leaders should be held accountable for their part of the partnership:

- Providing programming and structure that reflects the vision and plan for student spiritual

development—to lead students to KNOW God, OWN their faith, and make their faith KNOWN.
- Providing a curriculum map that covers the six years of student ministry with a balanced approach to spiritual development.
- Providing events that are strategic in nature and contribute to spiritual development.

Here are just a few practical ideas that you can use to help and support parents.

Meet with the pastoral staff.—Make sure your pastor understands your heart for parents and your perspective on helping parents serve as the primary spiritual developers in the lives of their students.

Enlist parents for a short-term study.—Spend four to six weeks teaching parents what it means to be the primary spiritual developer in the lives of their students. The best time I have found to do this is on Sunday mornings. Offer this class at least twice a year. (See Appendix 2, "Recommended Resources," p. 122 for suggested resources.)

Present the Parent Partnership as a part of the study.—Use the final week of the study to present the Parent Partnership. Help parents begin to understand what your respective roles and responsibilities will be in the future.

Hold a commissioning service for parents.—At the conclusion of the study, conduct a commissioning service on a Sunday morning or evening.

Many churches hold a baby/parent dedication as a part of a worship service. This is a special time when parents stand in front of the congregation, and the parents and the church affirm their respective responsibilities in helping the child grow up in a godly environment.

Plan a similar dedication service for parents of teenagers. There is never a better time for parents to recommit to the parenting process than when their children are entering adolescence! Parents can commit themselves to serve as the primary spiritual developers in the lives of their students. (An added benefit is that parents in the congregation could be encouraged and challenged to step up and go through the next study around the Parent Partnership process.)

SAMPLE PARENT PLEDGE

Parents: We pledge to assume the role of primary spiritual developer in the life of our student. We promise to provide a home that will reflect the teachings of Jesus Christ and allow our student to see what a home centered in Christ looks like. We promise to follow the principles in Deuteronomy 6 and create experiences in the home that will point our student toward a godly life.

Church: We pledge to encourage and support parents in their role as primary spiritual developers. We promise to help our church be a place that is family friendly and allows the family to come first.

Provide parents with support resources.—Make sure you are resourcing parents throughout this process. There are a variety of resources available in books, magazines, and online. Provide parents with resources for both their personal use and time with their students. (See Appendix 2, "Recommended Resources," p. 122 for suggested resources.)

Plotting Progress in the Partnership

Is there a way to measure our progress in this partnership? Quantifying spirituality is a lot like nailing Jell-O® to the wall! But if we are moving forward with a process of spiritual development, then there should be some measurable results.

Create a report card that can be used with your parents during a monthly or quarterly meeting. Place on the card those things the parents have agreed to do. Include a place for them to record the spiritual conversations they are having with their students. Include a place for them to record times of prayer they are having with their students. Leave an area blank for them to write in any opportunities that they have taken advantage of during the month so they can begin writing their own story of spiritual development.

This is not for the purpose of grading them, but strictly for the purpose of accountability and sharing.

After the cards are filled out, allow parents time to share about what has been going on in their homes. This is a great opportunity for parents to encourage each other!

This quarterly meeting is also your opportunity to be accountable to parents. Share with them where you are in your curriculum plan for the year. Let them see how it matches up with your strategy. Preview any events you will be doing the next quarter, and show them how those match up with the strategy.

Sample Parent Report Card

Activity/Week	Week 1	Week 2	Week 3	Week 4
Prayed for my student Notes*:	☐ Yes ☐ No	☐ Yes ☐ No	☐ Yes ☐ No	☐ Yes ☐ No
Held a spiritual conversation with my student Notes*:	☐ Yes ☐ No	☐ Yes ☐ No	☐ Yes ☐ No	☐ Yes ☐ No
Spent time in personal devotion Notes*:	☐ Yes ☐ No	☐ Yes ☐ No	☐ Yes ☐ No	☐ Yes ☐ No
Made use of teachable moments Notes*:	☐ Yes ☐ No	☐ Yes ☐ No	☐ Yes ☐ No	☐ Yes ☐ No

*Allow additional space for notes.

Now What?

Your plan is now in place, . . . so go and may God be with you! Yeah right. That's kind of like being thrown into the water at age six and being told there is only one option! We'll try to be a little more helpful than that.

Read on. The next chapter will help you get organized and consider ways to implement this strategy in your student ministry.

CHAPTER 5

IMPLEMENTING A KNOWN STUDENT MINISTRY

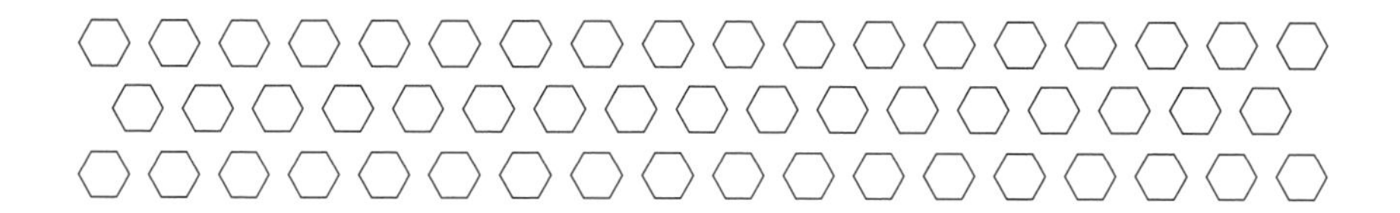

THE PROBLEM WITH MOST STRATEGIES is not in their creation but in our implementation. It's easy for us to come up with creative ways to identify what we want to do, then develop multimedia presentations to demonstrate our strategic expertise. The struggle seems to come with implementing our strategies and forcing them to affect what we do on a daily basis. If our strategies do not affect what we do in ministry, then they become nothing more than impressive presentations and good ideas at best. They live a short life of a few showings, then end up sitting in a notebook doing nothing more than taking up shelf space.

If we believe Luke 2:52 gives us a picture of Jesus' development, then we have no choice but to make sure that our ministries mirror that picture. We've already said that our focus needs to be on the spiritual development of students and not our student ministries, but here's the catch: the vehicle we've been given to support spiritual development *is* our student ministry.

So how do we create a ministry that leads students to KNOW God, OWN their faith, and make their faith KNOWN?

What Does a KNOWN Student Ministry Look Like?

Works through the home and the church.—A KNOWN student ministry is carried out through the two God-given institutions of the church and the home. You have seen this phrase throughout the book because it's important that we balance these two ministries. Using Deuteronomy 6 as a model for discipleship, we need to make sure the ministry we are providing through the church is supporting the ministry that should be happening in the home.

Focused on the individual.—A KNOWN student ministry values the development of individual students over the development of student ministry as a whole. It's very easy to organize our ministries so that our programmatic elements are in place and our events are planned. We need to consider the impact of those programs and events on the individual.

Programs with balance.—Programming by itself is not the answer. There are a lot of churches busy with great events and programs, but they have the same problem as churches with little or no programming—a 70-75 percent dropout rate among their graduating seniors.

Part of the solution is balance. Programming needs to be balanced. It needs to impact the whole individual, touching the students' relationship with God, self, and others (family, friends, authorities, and so forth). It needs a balance of upward, inward, and outward development.

The What and Why of Organizing

If we want students to KNOW God, OWN their faith, and make their faith KNOWN, we need to organize and plan strategically. There are a variety of ways to carry out this strategy for spiritual development. There is not one preferred way to organize, because there are a variety of factors that will shape your organization.

Church culture.—Every church operates in its own culture. Your church's culture is built around what the church family values.

For example, I (Jeff) served in a First Baptist Church in a county-seat town in Georgia. We were having a discussion over what time on Sunday we were going to hold a contemporary service. As we discussed the options of 9:15 a.m. or 11:00 a.m., one of the members asked, "Pastor, if we have a contemporary service at 11:00 a.m., will we become known as a contemporary church?"

I told him that most Southern Baptist churches are known for what they do at 11:00, so there was the possibility that we could become known as a contemporary church.

He quickly answered back that he did not think our church wanted to lose its heritage and history of being a strong traditional Southern Baptist church. All of the members of the church council quickly agreed, and we made our decision. It didn't matter if it was better or worse for any particular group of people we were trying to reach. Church culture drove the decision.

You can attempt to change church culture, but just know that many good people have died trying! Culture is not a good thing or a bad thing, it is just the context in which you minister. I would encourage you, before you accept a position of ministry, that you have an understanding of the church culture. It will save you from a lot of headaches and heartaches in the long run.

So as we look at organizational structure, we will not talk about *when* you do something as much as we will talk about the *what* and *why*. The "when" will be determined by your church's cultural lens.

Classification.—With each program or event you implement, you will want to consider how it helps carry out the strategy. Is this event designed to help students KNOW God, OWN their faith, or make their faith KNOWN?

This is where it gets tricky. Remember the focus is on the individual. That means a single small-group Bible study may impact different students in different ways. One student may be challenged to KNOW God, because she is drawn to know Christ and accept Him as her Savior and Lord. Another individual is moved to OWN his faith as he discerns the difference between what Christ said and what the world teaches. And a third individual chooses to make his faith KNOWN, because he sees how he can take that same truth and share it with a friend.

Nevertheless, there is value in identifying the *primary* function or purpose for each occasion. Identifying a primary purpose does not dismiss the different ways God can touch lives through a program or event, but it does help us to plan strategically. Were we to conclude that *every* event helps students KNOW God, OWN their faith, and make their faith KNOWN, we could lose focus on what we want to accomplish through that event. Losing focus leads to losing balance.

Yes, the focus of the KNOWN strategy is on the individual, but we can also think strategically about the group. (See "Implementing a KNOWN Student Ministry," p. 102.)

Building Intentionality into Our Meeting Times

Most student ministries have multiple occasions when they meet together during the week.

- For most churches, Sunday morning is still the prime meeting time: Sunday School (or Bible study or small groups) followed or preceded by a churchwide corporate worship service.
- Many churches continue to meet on Sunday evenings. This may be a time of discipleship, fellowship, or a combination of the two. Other churches choose another night during the week for some form of small-group Bible study. They may meet some place else like homes or schools.
- Many student ministries include some type of midweek event. If you live in the Bible belt, students

likely gather for some type of worship and/or Bible study on Wednesday nights. Other churches meet on another night during the week.

Church culture and regional culture may create other opportunities for you. For simplicity's sake, we are going to think in terms of the three types of occasions noted above. Where your church setting differs, think creatively to see how the organizational principles presented can be applied and adapted to your own setting.

Here are two examples of how different churches *without* a strategy might schedule their weekly youth gatherings:

First Church Bible Belt

Day	Time	Purpose
Sunday	9:45 a.m.	Bible study
	11:00 a.m.	Corporate worship
	6:00 p.m.	Discipleship
	7:00 p.m.	Fellowship
Wednesday	6:00 p.m.	Bible study

Progressive Fellowship

Day	Time	Purpose
Sunday	10:00 a.m.	Corporate worship
Tuesday	7:00 p.m.	Student worship
Friday	7:00 p.m.	Discipleship

Now it's your turn. Go to the chart on page 100 and write down the occasions that your student ministry meets and the main purpose of each meeting. Fill in just the first three columns for now (Day, Time, and Purpose).

Opportunities for Students to KNOW God

How do we help students KNOW God? This should be the primary function of corporate worship and community groups.

Corporate worship.—The cornerstone of helping students know God intimately is their involvement in corporate worship. Worship is the opportunity for us to connect with God personally and intimately. As personal as that is, it can happen even as we meet corporately.

Churches utilize a variety of approaches to student worship. Some churches limit those times to worship with the entire church body, and other churches create worship services for students only. There is value in both churchwide worship and student-only worship.

Those who would speak against the systematic segregation of students for the purpose of spiritual development would say that we have become isolationist. They would argue that because students don't participate with children and adults in church life and worship, we have given them a distorted view of the Christian life and their responsibility to the body of Christ. We do know that encouraging students to worship with the whole body will help them stay connected and less likely to drop out after graduation.

This is not to say that providing a time for student worship is wrong or spiritually unhealthy. Students need opportunities to express worship within their own adolescent cultural context. The key is to strive for balance.

Check the balance of worship opportunities for your students by answering the following questions.

- When are you providing an opportunity for your students to be involved in corporate worship with the entire church body?
- Are students active participants in the corporate worship service?
- If you have a student-only worship time, are students encouraged to participate in both services? Is there a scheduling conflict?
- If you have a separate worship service for students, what is its spiritual foundation?
- Do students invite their friends to attend one or both services?

Community groups.—A community group is when students gather each week to study the Bible. This is some type of open group setting, one in which students can join at any time. If a student misses one week, he or she can come back the following week and not feel lost in what's being studied. It is a group to which students can invite other students—their community—to come and be involved. The community group is an entry point to your student ministry.

For many student ministers, Wednesday night is their community group setting, their entry point to student ministry. Other student ministers would consider Sunday morning Bible study (Sunday School) as the entry point and community group setting. *When* is not the issue; what matters is that you have community groups!

Look at your organizational structure on page 100 and identify your community group meeting. Where are you offering students their first exposure—this open-door opportunity—to come into your ministry? Consider these questions to help you identify your community group.

- To which event do your students typically invite their unchurched friends?
- Which event is based on Bible study that could be understood even if a student wasn't present the previous week?
- Are your community groups designed to assimilate students into the full life of you church?

Opportunities for Students to OWN Their Faith

There are many ways you can help your students OWN their faith, but that is a primary function of covenant groups. Covenant groups are unique from community groups for several reasons. Covenant groups lend themselves to a more intentional approach to discipleship. They also tend to be more intense in their approach to spiritual development.

Covenant groups are usually closed groups. They meet for a set duration with the same group of students each week. Because of the nature of the topic and how each study builds on the previous one, it is difficult for new students to join the group once it is underway. Because a closed covenant group is not having to reintroduce the topic to new students each week, the members of the group have time to dig a little deeper into the subject. Often these groups include study outside of meeting times and increased accountability. The goal is to lead students into a better understanding of who they are in Christ. In other words, OWNing their faith.

Look at your current structure on page 100. Answer the following questions to help you determine when you are meeting in covenant groups.

- At which event do you offer deeper Bible study that is best understood with consistent attendance?
- At which event do you offer short-term Bible studies for a set number of meetings?
- At which event do you offer Bible study that requires participants to do work outside of class?
- At which of your events are the groups intentionally smaller?

Some student ministers are strong advocates for community groups, making statements such as: "Our whole student ministry is built around Sunday School" or "Everything begins and ends with Wednesday night." Other student ministers are advocates for covenant groups, saying: "Everything we do grows out of our small groups." Don't lose sight of the goal: a *balanced* approach to student spiritual development. If your Wednesday night event and Sunday morning event are both serving the same purpose (for example, community groups), then you should consider one of these options:

1. Change the purpose and focus of one of these events to be a time for covenant groups; or
2. Find an additional meeting time when you can establish covenant groups.

My (Jeff) church was structured to provide our community group experience on Sunday mornings and our covenant group experience on Wednesday nights. However, our Wednesday nights were becoming more of a community group, so our leadership team decided to create a covenant group experience on Sunday nights. It is a smaller group of students, but these students are growing deeper in their faith.

Let your organizational structure be fluid. The organization needs to change as the dynamics of the youth group changes. Don't get stuck on times and dates; be committed to purpose and results.

Opportunities for Students to Make Their Faith KNOWN

If we're exposing students to Jesus Christ, and we're taking them deeper in their faith through covenant groups, then there needs to be outlets for them to live out what they're learning. All this can be accomplished through ministry groups.

Think beyond an event. A ministry group should meet on a regular basis. Ministry groups should serve people in the church, as well as people outside the church. They can bring together different people in the church. As a result, ministry groups can help students stay connected to the local church after graduation. LifeWay Research has found that the more a student is involved in serving in the local church, the greater likelihood there is of that student staying connected to the church after graduation.

Ministry groups should be ongoing. That is not to take away from short-term ministry events (like a mission trip), but we don't want events to become our only outlet for ministry. Such events can be a great way to introduce students to ministry. Get them started at those events, but give them opportunities to serve and minister on a regular basis.

Giving students the opportunity to participate in a consistent, regular ministry group helps them feel like they are making a long-term investment in something. This investment allows them to develop ministry relationships and see God's work over time. Find opportunities within the church for students to serve: AV production, ushers, or greeters, for example.

Develop groups that minister outside the church as well. These can be ongoing ministry opportunities such as ministry to a nursing home, ministry to underprivileged kids, or other service projects in your community. Provide options for a variety of interests and skills.

Look at your current structure on page 100. Answer the following questions to help you determine when you are providing opportunities to serve in ministry groups.

- What opportunities do students have to serve in your church?
- What opportunities do students have to serve their community through your student ministry?
- Do you only view mission opportunities in the context of one week out of the summer?
- Do you have an intentional missional strategy for your student ministry?

Evaluating Your Organizational Structure

Let's review.

- The primary purpose of corporate worship and community groups is to help students KNOW God.
- The primary purpose of covenant groups is to help students OWN their faith.
- The primary purpose of ministry groups is to help students make their faith KNOWN.

The operative word in all this is *balance.*

We are not prescribing *when* these occasions should happen. Just make sure they happen! Your church and community's schedules will help determine the most opportune times.

Let's go back and look at our sample churches again.

FBC Bible Belt

Day	Time	Purpose	Group
Sunday	9:45 a.m.	Bible study	Community
	11:00 a.m.	Corporate Worship	Community
	6:00 p.m.	Discipleship	Covenant
	7:00 p.m.	Fellowship	Community/ Covenant
Wednesday	6:00 p.m.	Bible study	Community

Progressive Fellowship

Day	Time	Purpose	Group
Sunday	10:00 a.m.	Corporate Worship	Community
Tuesday	7:00 p.m.	Student Worship	Community
Friday	7:00 p.m.	Discipleship	Covenant

How would you change these churches' schedules and organization to bring balance?

Now review your own schedule and determine what changes need to be made to bring balance. Use the chart on page 101 to create your strategic plan.

Events Based on Strategy

We know there's more to student ministry than just the weekly schedule. We plan additional events. We spend a lot of time and dollars on special events, but they should be strategic too.

The easiest thing to do is simply to grab our calendars, look at the different times of the year, and schedule events based on past tradition, success, or just an opportunity to have fun. Is there anything wrong with this? There is if your planning lacks strategy. All events should be strategically planned to do primarily one of three things:

- Help students KNOW God
- Help students OWN their faith
- Help students make their faith KNOWN

Is there time to just have fun? Sure there is. But we can have fun while being strategic!

A KNOW event is going to be primarily evangelistic in nature. It can be structured for your students to bring their lost friends, an event that will impact your community for Jesus Christ. These are events such as Youth Vacation Bible School, a youth revival, camp, or a youth evangelism conference.

OWN events are planned primarily to create and develop fellowship and community within the group. They're structured primarily for students currently involved in your student ministry, events that foster growing closer together and become a place where youth group traditions are established. These events could be carried out through a See You at the Pole event, True Love Waits event, leadership training weekend, in-depth Bible study retreat, and so forth.

KNOWN events are planned primarily for the purpose of serving others. They're structured for ministry but can be attended by both your students and their friends. These events could be carried out through short-term mission trips, local ministry projects, a witnessing training event, or other similar activities.

School breaks—winter, spring, and summer—are natural choices for planning multi-day mission experiences for students. For many students these become landmark experiences in their spiritual journey. (See Appendix 3, "Student Missions," p. 124 for recommendations on ministry providers who offer opportunities for mission experiences.)

Planning Strategically

Here's the scenario. There's a long weekend on the calendar, and nothing is planned. No school events, no church events, nothing. An ideal weekend for an event. On top of that, your students have loved DiscipleNow (DNow) retreats in the past, and they've asked for another one. Any student minister worth his or her weight in youth group T-shirts will figure out that long weekend would be a good time for a DNow retreat. Brilliant.

But this is where a student minister needs to think strategically. How does this fit his or her strategy? How does this DNow weekend help students KNOW God, OWN their faith, or make their faith KNOWN?

The DNow retreat could be a KNOW event. Choose a topic such as prayer, worship, or faith and build your weekend around that topic. Encourage your youth and their lost friends to attend.

The DNow retreat could also be an OWN event. Choose a study that provides an opportunity for youth to develop a more Christlike character or sharpen their discernment skills. This event could promote fellowship and community within the youth group.

If you plan the retreat this way, it may be more geared for the Christians in your group. That doesn't mean they can't invite their friends, or that a lost student can't find Christ at an OWN event. The intent in thinking strategically is to identify the *primary* purpose of the event.

The DNow retreat could be planned as a KNOWN event. For example, you could choose a curriculum that trains youth in how to share their faith. The retreat could include opportunities for students to serve in the community and actually witness to others.

(See Appendix 2, "Recommended Resources," p. 123 for DNow resource recommendations.)

The Big Picture

Don't just plan a DNow weekend. Plan it in light of your overall calendar. Bring balance to the picture. If you lean toward OWN events that deepen a student's faith, perhaps the DNow should be a KNOWN event, which would allow students to put that deepening faith into practice.

You're not just planning a single event. You are planning with the full year in mind. But let's go beyond that. Plan in light of the six years a student will pass through your student ministry.

You may have certain events you do annually, such as a DNow weekend, youth camp, mission trip, and fall retreat. These four events then become the cornerstone events that frame your ministry. But you must look at these events strategically. (See Appendix 3, "Student Camps," p. 125 for descriptions of LifeWay Student Camps.)

Here's one scenario:

- *Fall*—A retreat on learning how to think critically about media is an OWN event
- *Winter*—A DNow event that helps students KNOW God
- *Spring*—Spring break mission trip where students can make their faith KNOWN
- *Summer*—Youth camp that is a KNOW event for both Christians and non-Christians

Here's another scenario:

- *Fall*—School year kicks off with a leadership retreat, where students learn to influence others and make their faith KNOWN
- *Winter*—Ski retreat where students are challenged at night to KNOW God
- *Spring*—A DNow weekend focused on developing godly character and helping students OWN their faith
- *Summer*—MFUGE, which includes both a camp element where students can KNOW God and a missions element where students can make their faith KNOWN.

These are not your only events, but they provide a foundation around which other events might be built.

Pastors, church leaders, and parents will love this. A full calendar is one thing, but a strategically-planned calendar communicates that you are doing more than just finding ways to keep students busy and entertained. And come budget time (woo-hoo!), a strategically-planned calendar shows purpose in why you need *X* number of dollars for this event and that event, increasing the likelihood of getting the budget dollars you requested.

FROM THEORY TO PRACTICE

The true value of the KNOWN strategy is realized as it is implemented in a church setting, as it moves from theory to practice. Let's recap. A KNOWN Student Ministry:

- Works through the church and the home
- Focuses on the individual
- Programs with balance
- Meets with intentionality

We also learned that the gathering occasions in a KNOWN Student Ministry could be connected to their primary strategic function. These gatherings include:

- Corporate Worship & Community Groups—KNOW
- Covenant Groups—OWN
- Ministry Groups—KNOWN

We can plan our ministry events with purpose so that we offer a balanced approach to spiritual growth for our students. **A word of caution:** Be sure that the purpose of your meeting times and events matches your practice. In an effort to create the illusion of balance, it can be tempting to label a gathering something that it is not. Don't fall into that trap.

Now it's time to take the next practical steps to make the KNOWN strategy a reality in your current place of service.

Current Schedule for ______________________________
CHURCH NAME

When	What	Why	
Day	**Time**	**Purpose**	**Group**

1. Identify the community group meeting time that would be your entry point.
2. Identify when your students are being connected with the whole church through worship.
3. Identify the covenant group meeting time in which you are discipling your youth in a closed group.
4. List your opportunities for ongoing ministry groups
   Inside the church—

   Outside the church—

Strategic Schedule

Review your current schedule and determine what changes should be made to bring balance to your ministry gatherings. Use the chart below to create a balanced plan based on your church and community's schedules.

CHURCH NAME

When	What	Why	
Day	Time	Purpose	Group

1. List opportunities for ongoing ministry groups.

2. Identify the cornerstone events that frame your ministry.

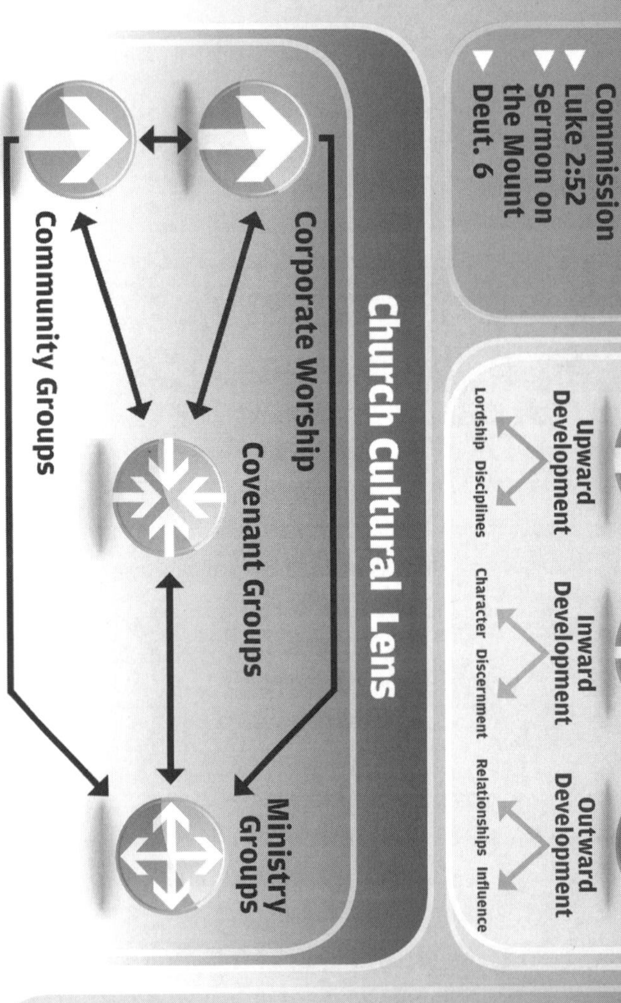
Implementing a KNOWN Student Ministry
Biblical Foundations
The Great Confession
The Great Commandment
The Great Commission
Luke 2:52
Sermon on the Mount
Deut. 6
Student Culture Lens
KNOW
OWN
KNOWN
Upward Development
Inward Development
Outward Development
Lordship
Disciplines
Character
Discernment
Relationships
Influence
Signs of Progress
Students will KNOW Christ as they exercise lordship and disciplines.
Students will OWN their faith as they grow in character and discernment.
Students will make their faith KNOWN as they develop in relationships and influence.
Church Cultural Lens
Corporate Worship
Covenant Groups
Ministry Groups
Community Groups

CONCLUSION

NEXT STEPS

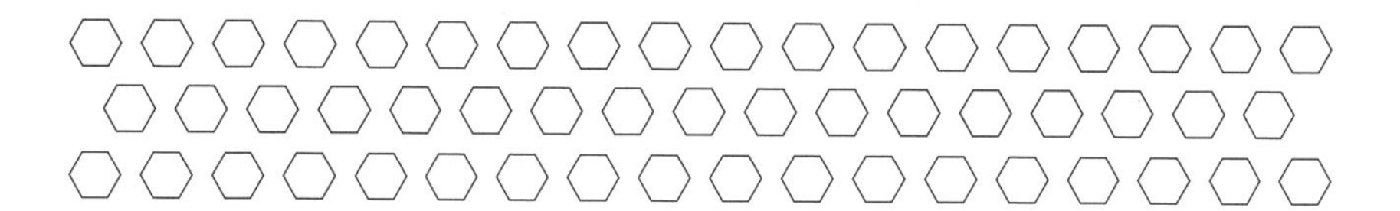

ONE OF THE BIGGEST CHALLENGES I (Scott) face after I've attended training seminars, read books and articles, watched videos, or just listened to others speak about different approaches to student ministry is trying to decide my next step. How do I apply the ideas I've heard to my present ministry situation? What are the transferable principles that can be used to increase ministry impact?

Over the course of this book we've presented a ministry strategy that is focused on the spiritual development of students. It is biblically based; its goal is for students to KNOW Christ, OWN their faith, and make their faith

KNOWN; and it is best carried out through the home and the church. As we conclude, let's think through some of the key factors to help connect the KNOWN strategy to your present place of service.

Ministry Context

The three churches I (Scott) served as a full-time student minister were located in a variety of ministry contexts. The first was a First Baptist Church located in a county seat town of six thousand in rural west Tennessee. The second was a First Baptist Church in an upper-middle class suburb, north of Houston, Texas. And the third was a First Baptist Church (beginning to notice a pattern?) located in a transitioning neighborhood near Dallas, Texas.

My basic student ministry philosophy was the same in each location, but how it was implemented was tailored to fit each particular ministry context. Just like the best Bible study experiences with students are those that are customized to their needs, a customized approach to implementing the KNOWN strategy is also needed. No one knows your church, community, students, leaders, and parents better than you. Here are a few factors to consider as you design a plan for your ministry context:

1. Setting.—Is it rural, urban, suburban, international? What is the pace of life like? Who are the people in your community? Is the population of your community reflected in the population of your church? What unique challenges and opportunities do you have for ministry to students, their families, your extended church family, and your community? What is the socio-economic environment, and how should this guide the types of programs, ministries, and activities offered?

2. *Resources.*—These can include people, money, and facilities. How can you maximize the ministry impact of your resources? How can you creatively overcome deficits in resources and include students in the process? How can you teach students about what is truly valuable through your deployment of the resources God has provided?

3. *Church Practice.*—What are the ongoing programs of your church and ministry? What about schedules? Is your church formal or informal? Traditional, contemporary, or blended worship? Any sacred traditions? How can the KNOWN strategy complement or strengthen your church?

4. *Schools.*—How many schools are represented in your student ministry? Public? Private? Home school? How do you create a sense of unity if students from several schools are present? (One suggestion is to categorize students by their high-school graduation year instead of their grade—even for middle school or junior high students. That way when they come to church they are always referred to as the Class of 2010, 2011, 2012, and so on.)

5. *Volunteer Leaders.*—Volunteers are essential for effective student ministry. These leaders should feel called by God to this role and must love Christ, the Bible, the church, and students. They should be able to communicate God's Word in both lessons and lifestyle. A robust sense of humor doesn't hurt! Their willingness to build relationships with students, parents, and other volunteers is crucial.

How's your team? Do you have a plan for recruiting and training new leaders? Is it time to de-enlist a leader?

6. Parent Participation.—How active are parents in the spiritual lives of your students and in the life of your church? If there is little to no involvement, how can you work with other church leaders and members to reach these parents for Christ? Student ministry belongs to the whole church—not on a separate youth ministry island—and ministering to parents is an area where the full force of the body of Christ is needed. Seasoned saints can also help bridge the gap by serving as effective spiritual mentors for students. A web of caring adult relationships with teens that includes parents, teachers, ministers, and mentors is the goal.

7. Students and their spiritual development.—What is the general level of spiritual interest and maturity in your students? What sort of issues are they dealing with? How serious are these issues? How unified is the group of students in your ministry? What are their greatest needs, spiritual and otherwise? What is the plan for them as they enter and as they exit your student ministry?

This is not an exhaustive list but hopefully it can spur your thinking as you develop a customized plan to implement the KNOWN strategy in your church. God, in His infinite wisdom, has called you to a particular ministry setting where your personality and gifts are being used to further His kingdom purposes. Our desire is that this strategy would be a tool to help you accomplish your mission.

First Steps

One of the most important steps in making sure that your plan becomes more than just a fancy multimedia presentation is to have an effective implementation strategy. Your goal must be to create a plan that will allow you to implement the KNOWN strategy . . . and keep your job at the same time! I (Jeff) came up during the seeker movement era and saw a lot of well-intentioned pastors lose their jobs and destroy good churches because they did not have a plan. For your plan to be effective, it must include communication, buy-in, and implementation.

COMMUNICATION

Ever feel like you are operating in seclusion and what you do really does not affect the rest of the church? The reality is that what we do *should* affect the rest of the church! We should see ourselves as partners with all facets of the church. Communication is essential to a successful partnership. Communicating with your pastor will allow you to accomplish several very important factors.

1. It will affirm your belief in his pastoral leadership. I (Jeff) hear from student ministers across the country, and it is not uncommon for them to meet with their pastors only once a month. Some pastors feel very comfortable with the leadership of their student ministers and do not feel the need to visit with them on a regular basis.

I have heard some pastors say they really do not understand their student minister. A meeting, then, would be awkward and unproductive. All the more reason to meet with your pastor and affirm your belief in his pastoral leadership in the church.

2. It will show your pastor that you actually have a plan. I cannot imagine anything being more pleasing to a pastor than to know that his student minister has a plan for ministry that stretches beyond the next youth camp, DiscipleNow, or the infamous winter lock-in. This is your chance to let your pastor see that you have a biblical foundation for student ministry and a strategy that will lead to the spiritual development of students. Your pastor has a heart for spiritual development—that's why he does what he does—so join his heart and show him that your passion is to see students develop into spiritually-mature adults.

3. It may start a revolution in your church. Student ministry is not the only area thinking strategically. Childhood Ministry at LifeWay has developed a strategy for childhood development around the terms *Hear, Know, Do.* Adult Ministry has a strategy for adult development around the terms Connect, Grow, Serve, Go.

Hopefully, your church is already thinking strategically about lifespan spiritual development "from birth to heaven," but if not, imagine yourself being a catalyst for the other age groups and ministries in your church. When you meet with your pastor, he may be inspired to develop a strategy for all areas of the church. A churchwide focus on spiritual development from birth to heaven would be great. And when the other groups are working and planning for spiritual development, it only helps and supports your work in student spiritual development. (See Appendix 4, "LifeSpan Spiritual Development," p. 127.)

4. It will justify your shift in student ministry practice. If you implement the strategies found in this book, it will change the way your student ministry looks and the way you interact with your students. As you begin to make curriculum changes, you now have a reason for that shift. When you make an adjustment to your event schedule, you will have a reason for the adjustment. When you find yourself spending more time with parents, you will have a purpose for those meetings. Leave behind the days of changing things "just because," and move forward with purposeful change.

BUY-IN

The KNOWN strategy is not merely your strategy; it should be the strategy of everyone who impacts the spiritual development of teenagers. Communicate with these people to secure their buy-in and shared ownership.

1. Parents.—The most important group of people you will lean on throughout your ministry are the parents of your students. They become your workers, your support team, and your best friends. Remember parents are the primary ministers to their students and you are partnering with them in this process.

Give parents a vision of what student ministry can become if we begin to follow a biblical model for student spiritual development. Parents will be thrilled you have a strategy and an intentional plan for student spiritual growth.

2. Volunteers.—Volunteers also need to buy-in to the strategy; it needs to become *their* strategy. Communicate the importance of the strategy and how it impacts their particular role in the student ministry. Probably most of your volunteers will be either Sunday School teachers or small-group leaders. They will want to know how this affects what they do in the classroom. Show them how the curriculum they use helps to carry out the strategy.

3. Students.—Our students are more capable than we give them credit, and they need to understand that what we are doing in student ministry has purpose and biblical foundations. Help them understand what it means to KNOW God, OWN their faith, and make their faith KNOWN. Help them see that they will accomplish this as they learn about lordship, disciplines, character, discernment, relationships, and influence.

IMPLEMENTATION

It is time to quit talking and start walking, but where do you start?

1. Own the strategy.—Take the KNOWN strategy and make it your own. Your church may already have three words that are used to describe its strategy for ministry. If it does, then see if you can plug in those words for KNOW, OWN, and KNOWN. If it makes sense and accomplishes the same goal, then you are in great shape. If not, or if your church does not have any kind of strategy, then use KNOW, OWN, and KNOWN. There is nothing magical about the words, but the principles of the strategy are biblical and timeless.

Create a purpose statement around these words, one that describes your student ministry in less than a minute.

Here is a sample purpose statement:

_______________________ Church's student ministry exists to partner with parents to help students KNOW God, OWN their faith, and make their faith KNOWN.

Create a statement that is memorable and descriptive of what you want to accomplish because it becomes the driving force for all you do. Put this statement everywhere: letterhead, business cards, the walls of your youth room, on your social media networks, and your Web site. Challenge your students to memorize it.

2. Begin with Sunday Mornings.—The easiest place to make a large impact in moving toward a strategic approach to the spiritual development of your students is in foundational Bible study. In most of our churches there is some form of small-group Bible study on Sunday mornings. Whenever your church holds its foundational Bible study, use a curriculum that supports the KNOWN strategy.

3. Meet regularly with parents.—Of all groups, parents are the ones who will most influence the effectiveness of the KNOWN strategy. Meet with them regularly, at least once a quarter. Schedule your meeting during a time when the majority of parents will already be at church. Use the meeting to inform, educate, and inspire.

Inform: Help parents see how you are implementing the strategy with their students. Go over the next quarter of topics that will be covered during your small-group Bible study and the area(s) of the strategy that it will emphasize. Talk to parents about the events you have planned during the next quarter and how they fit into the strategy.

It's also a good time to solicit any help you may need to accomplish the events that are planned for the upcoming quarter. Parents will be more willing to invest their time when they see the plan, purpose, and effect the event will have on their own students' spiritual development.

Educate: Help parents gain a better understanding of the culture their students are growing up in. Do your research and address topics that are relevant to student culture. This is a good opportunity to gain credibility in your role. Make this time interactive and not a lecture, leaving plenty of time for questions. You do not have to give the impression that you know all the answers—parents know better!—but you can let parents know you are doing all you can to understand their teenagers.

Inspire: It is amazing how many parents are going through the same things with their students, but they never talk about it with each other. Set aside 20 minutes of your meeting time to talk about common issues that parents deal with. Get your list of topics by asking parents to write down the top three areas related to raising their children they would like to hear discussed. Address one topic per meeting. Advertise the topic beforehand and let that draw parents to your meeting.

You don't always have to be the expert. Enlist parents who have already struggled through the issue with their students to share from their experience. Let parents talk about how they have dealt with (or would deal with) the issue. Parents teaching each other. You can move from being the educator to being the facilitator.

Conducting a well-planned meeting will help you build a strong army of support. Getting workers will never be a problem again. Why? Because parents will understand what you are trying to accomplish.

The Need for Spiritual Power

He said to me, "Prophesy concerning these bones and say to them: Dry bones, hear the word of the LORD! This is what the Lord GOD says to these bones: I will cause breath to enter you, and you will live. I will put tendons on you, make flesh grow on you, and cover you with skin. I will put breath in you so that you come to life. Then you will know that I am the LORD."

–Ezekiel 37: 4-6

The story of the Valley of Dry Bones would make for a great movie scene. Dry bones scattered across a desolate valley suddenly coming back to life! Add just the right sound and visual effects—very, very cool.

Here's the spiritual reality: ministry strategies, principles, and frameworks—no matter how well-conceived and developed—are in and of themselves . . . dry bones. They are powerless. What they need is the breath of God's Spirit to give them life and the power to impact lives for eternity. The KNOWN strategy for student spiritual development is a helpful ministry tool (a solid skeleton), but it, or any other plan, will never be a substitute for the powerful presence of God's Spirit on a church or student ministry and in the hearts of students, parents, and leaders.

What is the current spiritual climate of your church, your ministry, and your life? If you are enjoying a season of God's favor, let's join together in thanking Him for His grace and faithfulness. But if this is a dry season, are there actions, attitudes, or spiritual apathy that are keeping you, your ministry, or your church from experiencing God's fullest blessings?

The Value of Check-ups

Hopefully you are in the habit of scheduling regular check-ups when it comes to your physical health. It is a wise move and can uncover problems before they become serious. They are not always fun, but definitely necessary.

The same is true for our spiritual health. Do you regularly check up on this? One of the things I've (Scott) noticed over the years is that spiritually-transforming student ministries tend to be led by spiritually-transformed leaders. One of the most penetrating questions I've ever heard related to ministry came from Billy Beacham. Billy asked, "If God took His hand off your ministry, how long would it be before anyone noticed?" It's still painful to consider this possibility.

For me this was a reminder that I could plan and implement all kinds of student ministry activities and programs, but without God's hand on them, they would count for nothing. This is especially dangerous for people who have been involved in student ministry for a number of years. There can be a fine line between *confidence* in ministry and *arrogance* in ministry. My guess is most people who have been in student ministry for a while could plan a year's worth of "stuff" with one hand tied behind their back. But would those plans lead to significant spiritual results?

In an effort to gauge and improve spiritual health, here are a couple of diagnostic tools to help assess your current well-being and ministry performance. Approach them prayerfully and honestly, asking God to reveal any areas that may need attention. Take some time now to consider the following statements and questions.

Critical Minimum Personal Inventory

Instructions: Use the following questions to help evaluate your spiritual health. Circle the most appropriate response based on the following scale: 4 = Always, 3 = Usually, 2 = Sometimes, 1 = Seldom, 0 = Never

Abiding in Christ

I have a daily quiet time.

4 3 2 1 0

I try to make Christ Lord of my life.

4 3 2 1 0

I feel close to the Lord throughout the day.

4 3 2 1 0

I try to discipline myself.

4 3 2 1 0

I am aware that the Lord disciplines me.

4 3 2 1 0

Living in the Word

I read my Bible daily.

4 3 2 1 0

I study my Bible each week.

4 3 2 1 0

I memorize a verse of Scripture each week.

4 3 2 1 0

I take notes at least once a week as I hear, read, or study the Bible in order to apply it to my life.

4 3 2 1 0

Praying in Faith

I keep a prayer list and pray for persons and concerns on the list.

4 3 2 1 0

I have experienced a specific answer to prayer during the last month.

4 3 2 1 0

Each day my prayers include confession, praise thanksgiving, petition, and intercession.

4 3 2 1 0

Adapted from *Masterlife Day by Day Personal Devotional Guide* by Avery Willis, Jr.

A Personal Ministry Evaluation

1. How happy are you with your performance as a student ministry leader during the past six months?
2. Do you pray and plan regularly with other student ministry workers in your church?
3. When you teach, do you prepare all through the week, the night before, or not at all?
4. How much time and effort do you spend in reaching students for Christ?
5. How much time and effort do you spend building relationships with students?
6. Have you attended any student worker training in the past year?
7. When was the last time you did something new and innovative with your teenagers?

8. Do you attend church services regularly and encourage your students to do the same?
9. Do you tithe?
10. Are you praying regularly for the students and families you have been called to minister to?
11. What changes in your work can you make to reach new students for Christ?
12. Do you pray regularly with/for other church staff members?

So, how are you doing? I don't know about you, but I am so thankful that the Holy Spirit who brings conviction to my life about areas that need attention is the same Holy Spirit who enables me to walk with greater obedience. It's encouraging to know that God's power is available to us as we seek to advance in spiritual maturity.

Our Prayer for You

Our prayer is that this call to focus on the spiritual development of individual students by leveraging the God-given roles of the home and the church will result in increased ministry effectiveness. We long to see an ever-growing number of students come to know Christ as Savior, move to an ownership of their faith, and boldly make their faith known in the world. We live in challenging times and it will be exciting to see what God continues to do in and through this generation.

Thanks so much for your continued investment in the lives of students. Isn't it exciting to be called of God to minister to students and their families through the church? We get to be involved in their significant life events and have the privilege of helping guide students as they wrestle with some of life's toughest questions. Never underestimate the value of your influence. Your faithfulness in sharing the good news of God's love through Jesus Christ is making an eternal impact. We close with a verse that reflects the very heart of ministry with students.

We cared so much for you that we were pleased to share with you not only the gospel of God but also our own lives, because you had become dear to us.

–1 Thessalonians 2:8

Building KNOWN Students Survey (Sample)

Instructions: Rate each statement from 1-5 (with 1 = strongly disagree, 2 = disagree, 3 = neutral, 4 = agree, and 5 = strongly agree).

LORDSHIP Goal: Students will recognize and respond to the lordship of Christ.	1	2	3	4	5
1. Experience personal salvation.					
2. Walk with assurance of their salvation.					
3. Order their lives based on the lordship of Christ.					
4. Exhibit an understanding of each member of the Trinity.					
5. Seek God's will in daily decisions.					
6. Resist temptation in the power of Christ.					

DISCIPLINES Goal: Students will practice spiritual disciplines.	1	2	3	4	5
1. Develop a lifestyle of daily prayer.					
2. Develop the habit of daily Bible reading, meditation, and Scripture memory.					
3. Develop a lifestyle of worship.					
4. Identify and utilize their spiritual gifts.					
5. Manage the resources God has given them.					
6. Live consistently by faith in God.					

CHARACTER Goal: Students will develop and demonstrate Christ's character.	1	2	3	4	5
1. Seek to honor God through a lifestyle of holiness.					
2. Consistently display the fruit of the Spirit.					
3. Display honesty, integrity, and purity.					
4. Strive for excellence in all aspects of life.					
5. Develop a self-image based on who they are in Christ.					
6. Develop the heart of a servant.					

DISCERNMENT Goal: Students will make wise decisions.	1	2	3	4	5
1. Affirm Scripture as the authoritative guide for their life.					
2. Apply Scriptural principles to daily decisions.					
3. Assume responsibility for their decisions.					
4. Recognize true teaching from false teaching.					
5. Possess and articulate a biblical worldview.					
6. Recognize and avoid the negative aspects of peer pressure.					

RELATIONSHIPS Goal: Students will develop godly relationships.	1	2	3	4	5
1. Recognize and submit to proper authorities.					
2. Encourage and minister to fellow believers of all ages.					
3. Cultivate relationships with non-Christians.					
4. Support their families through love and acting responsibly.					
5. Strengthen and encourage their friends.					
6. Deal with conflict in a Christlike manner.					

INFLUENCE Goal: Students will make an intentional impact on others.	1	2	3	4	5
1. Actively participate in the life and ministry of the local church.					
2. Lead someone to faith in Christ.					
3. Participate in mission and ministry projects.					
4. Confront the culture with the love of Christ.					
5. Defend their faith and beliefs.					
6. Use their abilities and talents in evangelism.					

Recommended Resources

Chapter 4

Page 76.—One way LifeWay is helping parents engage their students in dialogue on what their students are learning in Bible study is by providing questions and discussion ideas. If you use *KNOWN, Life Focus, Life Focus Online,* or *Fuel Ignited* you will find parent helps in the curriculum. *Life Focus and Life Focus Online* are part of the Bible Studies for Life series. If your adult classes use this series, students and their parents study the same Scripture passages.

Page 77.—For a short-term study for parents, we recommend *Indelible Parenting: Keys to a Lasting Impression Leader Guide* and *Member Book* (LifeWay Press, 2008).

Page 79.—For resources for parents to use alone and with their students, we recommend:

- *30 Days: Turning the Hearts of Parents & Teenagers Toward Each Other* by Richard Ross (LifeWay Press, 2003).
- *Living with Teenagers.*—This monthly magazine features articles that are relevant to parenting today. If you are using the KNOWN curriculum, the articles in the magazine will correlate to whatever topic is being taught that month. It can be ordered on LifeWay's Dated Resource Order Form or at *www.lifeway.com/magazines.*
- *Heart Connex.*—This twice-a-week, electronic delivery provides devotions for parents to share with their students. Parents can get these for free at *www.lifeway.com/students.*

Chapter 5

Page 97.—For a DNow to help youth get to KNOW God through worship, we recommend *Live to Worship* and *Live to Worship Leader Guide* (LifeWay Press, 2008).

For a DNow with the purpose of helping youth Own their faith, we recommend *Leap and Leap Leader Guide* (LifeWay Press, 2009).

For a DNow to help youth make their faith KNOWN, we recommend *Show Who You Know* and *Show Who You Know Leader Guide* (LifeWay Press, 2008) or *Live It, Tell It* and *Live It, Tell It Leader Guide* (LifeWay Press, 2008).

Additional LifeWay products for short-term Bible studies:

KNOW

- *Experiencing God: Knowing and Doing the Will of God, Youth Edition Member Book* and *Leader Guide* (9 sessions)

OWN

- *My Identity in Christ, Student Edition Member Book* and *Leader Guide* (6 sessions, plus introductory session)
- *Jesus on Leadership: Becoming a Servant Leader, Student Edition Member Book* and *Leader Guide* (6 sessions)

KNOWN

- *MasterLife, Student Edition Member Book* and *Leader Guide* (12 sessions)
- *Share Jesus Without Fear: Students Reaching Students* (5 sessions)

Student Missions

In addition to the missions opportunities provided through LifeWay camps (see pp. 125-126), there are opportunities provided through the North American and International Mission Boards.

WORLD CHANGERS (North American Mission Board)
World Changers seeks to provide Christian youth and adults with opportunities to meet the physical and spiritual needs of others through practical learning experiences that teach servanthood and personal commitment to missions.

Groups are typically housed in local schools, churches, or college facilities. Breakfast and dinner are provided cafeteria-style at the lodging site. Lunch is provided at the work site by local churches. In preparation for the week, youth are required to complete an pre-project study based on the theme, including a local work project.

For more information go to *www.world-changers.net.*

YOUTH ON MISSION (International Mission Board)
Youth groups, team, and individual youth participants work with IMB field personnel on a mission project to accomplish the ministry needs of the missionary. Team leaders and individual youth are responsible for working out the logistics of getting to the field.

Project Group Leader is responsible for trip arrangements such as flight itineraries, visas, immunizations, travel insurance, pre-project study, and raising and taking the money for on-the-field costs to the missionary. Field personnel will arrange on-the-field meals, housing, and in-country transportation, if needed.

For more information go to *www.thetask.org.*

Student Camps

CENTRIFUGE

In addition to powerful worship every morning and evening, students will experience small-group Bible study and team-building recreation led by highly-trained FUGE staffers. In the meantime, adults have the chance to refresh and fellowship with leaders from other churches through adult Bible study and recreation. Afternoon track times give everyone the opportunity to participate in a favorite activity or learn something new. Every part of the day is planned and executed by our FUGE staff so you don't have to worry about preparing for the next activity—you can focus on building relationships with students.

MFUGE

Roll your sleeves up and get ready to jump right into ministry. Our FUGE staffers will take care of the details, facilitating and planning each day. You and your students can invest your time and energy into mission projects. During the day students are challenged and stretched as individuals; in the evenings, you can build group unity over dinner, worship, fellowships, and church group devotions. MFUGE continues to partner with organizations in local communities to serve people in need. A portion of the missions offering is invested back into these communities to develop the ministries throughout the year.

XFUGE

Get the flexibility of doing your own camp, but save some time and energy in the planning process with XFUGE. We'll take care of all the big stuff: camp pastor, worship band, fun fellowships, lodging, food, and even Bible study curriculum. Your group joins everyone in the morning and evening for camp-wide services and fellowships, then you get to choose your experience for the rest of the day: participate in on-campus team-building options or head out for some group adventures. You also get to lead your group in the study and discussion of God's Word (curriculum provided by FUGE). XFUGE is available at ALL Combo Camp locations.

XFUGE ON MISSION

Combine the heart of missions with the elements of camp. Every morning starts with worship before your group heads off to a ministry site chosen just for you. XFUGE on Mission gives your students the opportunity to serve side by side and build group unity. You also get to lead your group in the study and discussion of God's Word (curriculum provided by FUGE). XFUGE on Mission is available at ALL MFUGE and Combo Camp locations.

FUGE COMBO CAMP

At a FUGE Combo Camp, church groups can choose from Centrifuge small-group Bible study, MFUGE ministry options, or the flexibility of XFUGE and XFUGE on Mission. Combo Camp participants will be together for portions of the day. Whatever combination you choose, an unforgettable summer is in store for you!

FUGE WINTER CAMP

Featuring excellent speakers, gifted worship leaders, and flexible daytime activities on campus or on the slopes of nearby Ski Santa Fe, FUGE Winter Camps at Glorieta Conference Center will challenge you to grow in your walk with Christ and allow you to have a whole lot of fun too!

These camps are for students entering grades 7-college and adult leaders.

Register at *www.lifeway.com/fuge* or 877-CAMP123

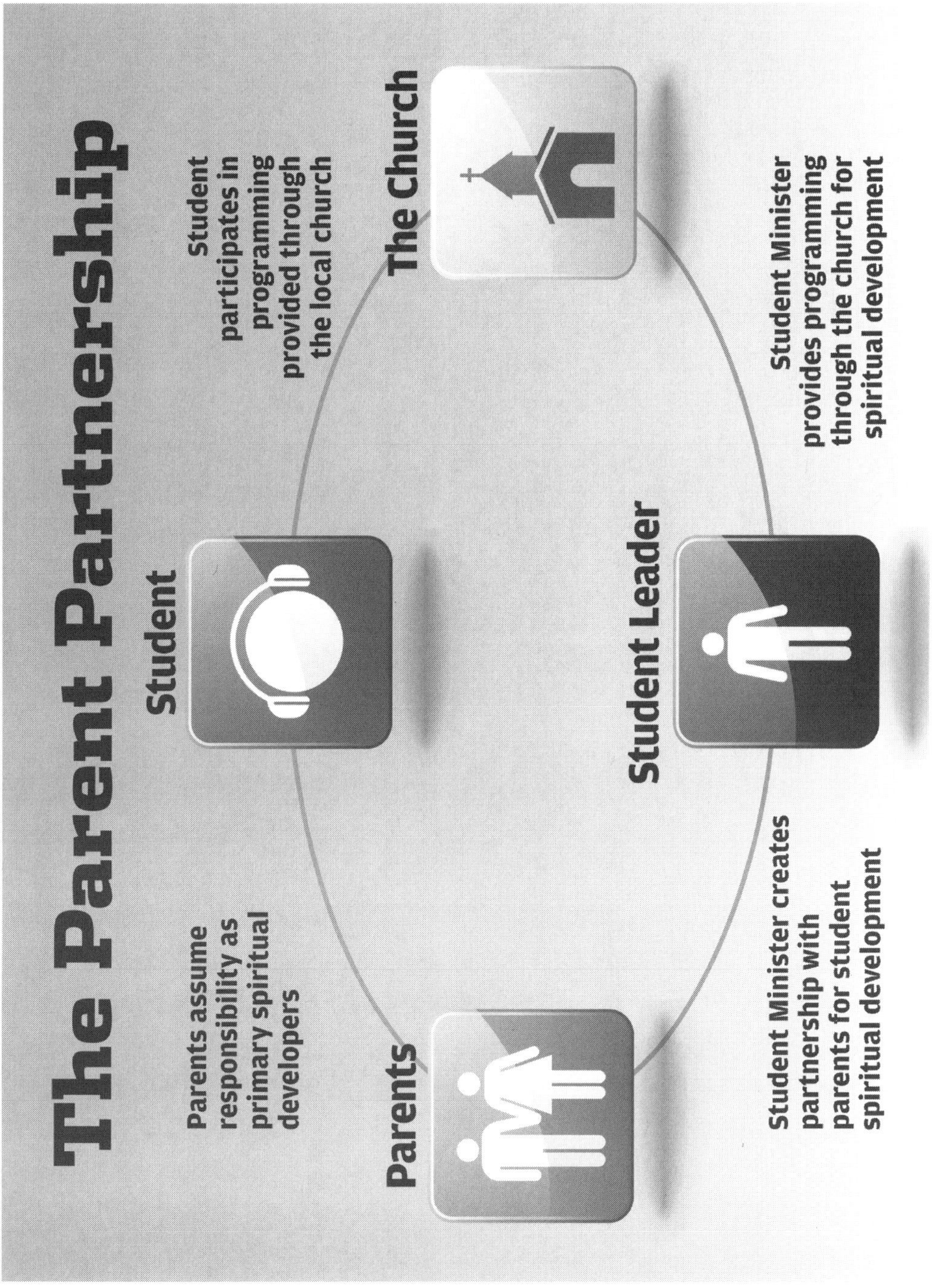

The Parent Partnership

Student

Parents assume responsibility as primary spiritual developers

Student participates in programming provided through the local church

Parents

The Church

Student Leader

Student Minister creates partnership with parents for student spiritual development

Student Minister provides programming through the church for spiritual development

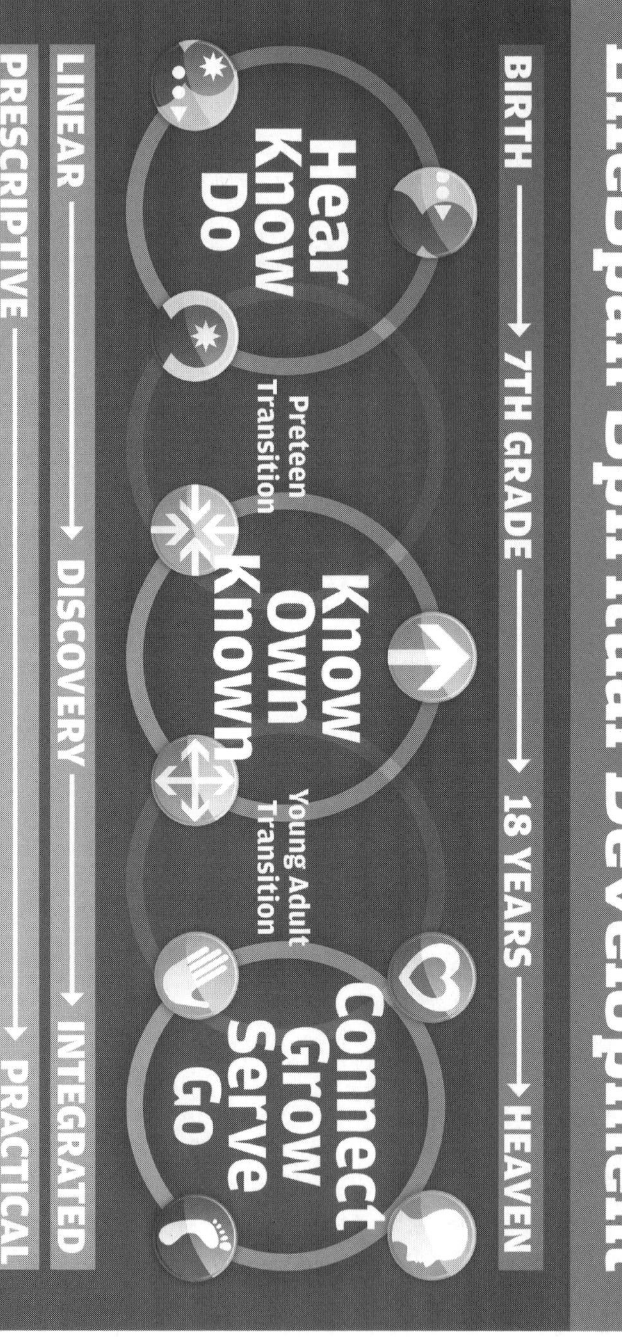
LifeSpan Spiritual Development
BIRTH → 7TH GRADE → 18 YEARS → HEAVEN
Hear Know Do
Preteen Transition
Know Own Known
Young Adult Transition
Connect Grow Serve Go
LINEAR → DISCOVERY → INTEGRATED
PRESCRIPTIVE → PRACTICAL
Prescriptive/Linear
Learning occurs through prescriptive levels of biblical learning that are taught in a very linear approach, providing the foundation for salvation and spiritual transformation.
www.lifeway.com/kidspromise
Linear/Discovery
Spiritual development occurs as students know God through lordship and disciplines, their own faith through character and discernment, and make their faith known through relatioinships and influence. The process is linear allowing for discovery through experience.
www.lifeway.com/studentstrategy
Discovery/Integrated
Spiritual growth occurs incrementally and concurrently as adults ineract with the 15 biblical concepts that impact with their personal experiences and practical life situations. Learning should integrate connecting, growing, serving, and going in balanced spiritual development.
www.lifeway.com/adultstrategy